JEFF SMITH

How To
Make More Profit With Your
Service Department

The ultimate guide to understanding and improving your operational efficiencies.

YOURS TO HAVE AND TO HOLD BUT NOT TO COPY

© 2003 Insight Training & Development Limited.

This publication is protected by copyright law. All rights are reserved. No portion of this book may be reproduced or used in any form – graphic, electronic or mechanical including photocopying, sound recording, information storage and retrieval systems, or by any other means without the written permission from the publisher.

Published by:

Insight Training & Development Limited
P. O. Box 1234
Stourbridge
England
DY8 2GE

Telephone:	0044 (0)1384 371432
Web Address	www.AskInsight.com
Email:	KPI@AskInsight.com

The right of Jeff Smith to be identified as the author of this work has been asserted by him in accordance with the Copyright, Designs and Patents Act 1988. "The Law Of The Service Department" wording, titles and diagrams are protected by international Trade Marks and copyright law and are for the exclusive use of Jeff Smith.

First printed in the UK 2003 by RPM Reprographics.

Dedicated to my three girls.
Sharon, Sophie and Lara

I love you more than anything.
(and you can't beat that!)

About The Author

Jeff Smith is regarded by many as one of the UK's leading business improvement strategists. He is particularly well known for his ability to convey complex information into jargon-busting, plain English that everyone understands.

As well as being one of the motor industry's top trainers and consultants, in 1999 he became a founder member of the Professional Speakers Association of Europe, he's appeared many times as a Motor Industry expert on Sky Television and he's also the author of The K.P.I. Book, the ultimate guide to understanding the key performance indicators of your business.

Jeff's career spans more than 20 years within the Motor Industry. He began his career in the Sales Department, progressed through to become Dealer Principal and then to Divisional Director within a retail motor group. He is proud to say that it was within these positions that he was able to develop his skills in Sales, Aftersales and Business Management.

He continued his career by becoming a Consultant to the Motor Industry and during this time he's worked with many car, truck and paint manufacturers around the world helping them to develop their profit improvement programmes within Sales, Service, Parts, Bodyshop and Business Management.

Jeff is the Managing Director of Insight Training & Development Limited which is based in central England where he runs his business with a team of associates who specialise in the Motor Industry. He also speaks at universities, product launches and conferences all over the world.

You are welcome to contact him directly by email with any questions you may have regarding the Motor Industry on JeffSmith@AskInsight.com

If you or your Managers would like to attend one of Jeff's Master Classes or you would like to arrange a training event or consultancy visit at your business, please contact his office on 0044 (0)1384 371432.

Acknowledgments

There is no such thing as a self-made man. Everyone needs help from other people to get things done and this book is no exception.

It has taken twenty years of experience, five years of research and a further two years of writing to complete this book and there are many people I wish to thank who have helped me along this journey.

Firstly, I'd like to thank the many Dealer Principals, Directors, Aftersales Managers, Service Managers, Franchise Directors and training course delegates who have shared your ideas with me. You have been willing to implement new ideas into your businesses and feedback the results to ensure that the initiatives contained in this book are practical solutions that actually work in the real world. There are too many people to mention by name, but you know who you are. This book is all about *you* and the successes that you have achieved. A million thanks to you all.

I'd also like to thank all of the vehicle manufacturers in the Motor Industry that have provided me with privileged and confidential information about their working practices and development strategies for the future. Your help in identifying best practice across your dealer networks has been invaluable. Thank you for taking me into your confidence.

I have family, friends and colleagues around the world who I would like to thank because you have always been there when I needed you. Over the past two years some of you have helped me by reading specific chapters to make sure that they were heading in the right direction and you gave me your honest opinions. Your comments have been more valuable than you can imagine. I wish to thank my friends who have assisted me with the final stages of proof reading; I admire your tenacity and patience, you have done a brilliant job. Others have helped by leaving me with words of inspiration and giving your continued moral support, sometimes unknowingly. My special thanks go to these people: Michel Remy, Bernard Gonnet, Mogens Nielsen, Trevor Davies, RAB Lee, Martin Kerr, Allan Hughes, Belinda and Shaun Davies, Gavin Hall, Mary and John Davies, Clare Scammell, Professor Garel Rhys OBE and of course my wonderful daughters Sophie and Lara and my mom and dad, Evelyn and Tom Smith.

And finally…there is one person who deserves all of the credit for this book; my wife Sharon. I travel all over the world developing consultancy and training projects and somewhere in between I write books and it is you that holds everything together. This book would not have been written if were not for your unconditional love and support. You never complain when I ask you to read stuff that you don't understand and you always have something positive to add. You are the one that keeps me on track and you have made many sacrifices yourself to allow me the time to write this book. You are my raison d'être and I am blessed to have you in my life.

Thank you.

Foreword
By Nick Fry - Honda Racing F1 Team

Winning in motor racing is no different to winning in any other business. Trust me, I have experienced both!

Having been lucky enough to spend over 25 years in the Motor Industry doing everything from running a car-a-minute body shop and assembly plant to building a dealer network, strategy planning and providing technical assistance to dealer Service Departments, I can say with authority that the basics are all the same, whatever the business.

I can't claim to have any unique insights but I have been lucky enough to have had some of the best teachers in the motor business and here is some of what I've learned.

First, have a strategy. If you don't know where you are or where you want to be, then action may make you feel good but you could be doing completely the wrong thing. Stop! The text books call it "current state analysis" or other fancy titles but all it means is find out where you are, what's wrong and what's right. Normally it's not half as bad as it might seem but if it is, don't despair. Make a list and work through it, one by one. Dull, but effective. But first, establish where you want to be. BHAG's are good. That's Big Hairy Audacious Goals.

When setting your goals, try to identify best practise but don't try to reinvent the wheel. Be realistic, understand your own limitations and exploit other peoples' ideas. No one has a lifespan long enough to discover everything themselves by trial and error. It would take far too long, cost far too much money and you would end up at the back of the grid. We all need to use other people's ideas and find ways of applying them and making them work to deliver better results in our own businesses.

Jeff Smith has done a fantastic job of capturing Service Department strategy and best practise in this book; it contains everything you need to achieve greater success. All the ideas are here in black and white; I urge you to read them, get excited by them, decide which ideas are right for you and then get busy, set your goals and take action!

If the goal is particularly daunting, one good technique is to pretend in your mind that you've already achieved your goal and then tell yourself how you achieved it. It's much easier looking back at what you've achieved (even if it's only in your mind) than only seeing obstacles in front of you.

Next, review the consequences of failure. If you can live with them, go full steam ahead. If not, think again.

Next step is to be bold. Only a fool keeps repeating the same thing and expecting a different outcome. Nothing will change unless you change something. So get going and don't mess around the edges. If a Formula One car isn't quick, no amount of playing with the suspension set up is going to make that much difference. Big problems need big changes so don't dilly-dally around.

Once you have set out on your chosen course, don't be afraid to change direction if it's not working. Keep talking to the people involved, find out what's going well and what needs improvement, keep looking at the metrics and get into the detail.

People hate giving bad news and will often dress up the good bits and downplay the bad. Don't shoot the messenger, listen, learn and react positively. Find out what is happening and make on-course-adjustments. Things rarely work out first time so don't be too proud to say "well that didn't work, what do we do next?" even when it was your idea. That will earn more respect than ploughing on regardless.

Lastly, remember the race never ends. I have heard too many times from teams who have achieved a 20% efficiency improvement year-over-year that it's impossible to do the same the following year. If you don't, someone else will.

You can't sit on your laurels; you have to continue striving for improvements in every area no matter how big or small. The moment you slow down, someone else will overtake you.

Within the Honda Racing F1 Team we have around 500 totally dedicated people who work flat out all year round, day and night, in an attempt to get two cars onto the starting grid of a Grand Prix. All of the other teams on the grid are doing the same thing and we are all striving to win. When you see the Formula One cars lined up on the grid on a Sunday afternoon you are witnessing the combined efforts of around 10,000 people, multi-£Billions of investment in that year alone and yet it is incredible to think that 1mm in ride-height on a car can make the difference between winning and losing that race.

In the last five years, a Formula One engine has gone from 750 to 950 bhp at the same time as reducing in weight from 130 to 90 kg at the same time as increasing its life from 400 to 1500 km. If we can do that with Formula One racing car, so can you with your Service Department!

Nick Fry
Chief Executive Officer
Honda Racing F1 Team

How To Use This Book

This is not a book where you start at the beginning and finish at the end; you choose the sections that are most relevant to your development at the time. For people with less than five years experience in the Service Department, it is recommended that you read Part I then Part III and then Part II.

PART 1
UNDERSTANDING YOUR
OPERATIONAL EFFICIENCIES

This section gives you the full understanding of your operational efficiencies written in jargon-busting plain English which include Utilisation, Productivity and Overall Efficiency. Once you understand each one of these areas you can then read Chapter IV, The Law Of The Service Department. This chapter explains how your operational efficiencies work with and against each other.

PART 2
HOW TO IMPROVE YOUR
OPERATIONAL EFFICIENCIES

This is the largest section and is probably the main reason for you buying the book. It contains over 100 tried and tested initiatives on how you can improve your Utilisation and Productivity. Each idea carries its own space so that you can record your comments and thoughts on how you can implement the concept into your business. At the end of each chapter you will find a quick reference check list so that you can keep track of your progress. You will notice that some initiatives affect both Utilisation and Productivity, but in slightly different ways. Only two or three of the initiatives have been repeated in the book and it is your challenge to identify the other ideas that will affect both areas of performance.

It is strongly recommended that you keep a record of your actions and if you do not wish to write in this book, then keep a separate record. In time, you will be able to look back at your work and make further improvements as you gain more experience.

Important note: Do not read any more than three of the initiatives at any one time. If you continue reading many of the ideas will merge in your mind and some important concepts may be lost. This book is about reading and then taking action; not just reading.

PART 3
CALCULATING THE GAIN IN YOUR OPERATIONAL EFFICIENCIES

This section contains all of the mathematics you need for budgeting and forecasting the effects of your actions. Although it is contained in the latter part of the book, it is recommended that you know how to accurately monitor your business before you attempt to implement new ideas into your business. As the old saying goes, if you cannot measure it, you cannot manage it. Understanding cause and effect is critical to your success.

THE READERS FORUM

You can find more support information and practical tips from other readers relating to the ideas contained in this book at www.AskInsight.com/service96.html

*"Darwin got it wrong.
It's not the survival of the fittest,
it's the survival of the most adaptable."*

- Jeff Smith

Contents

	Page
Introduction	1

Part 1
Understanding Your Utilisation	11
Understanding Your Productivity	19
Understanding Your Overall Efficiency	31
The Law of The Service Department	45

Part 2
How To Improve Your Utilisation	63
- Quick Reference Checklist	126
How To Improve Your Productivity	129
- Quick Reference Checklist	188

Part 3
Calculating The Gain In Your Utilisation	195
Calculating The Gain In Your Productivity	223
Where To Now?	247
How To Order Additional Copies	253
Books By Jeff Smith	254

INTRODUCTION

*"The man who views the world at 50
the same as he did at 20 has wasted
30 years of his life"*

- Muhammad Ali

INTRODUCTION

The Service Department produces high levels of profitability from its activities and for decades it has been the unrecognised backbone of a franchised dealership. Since the introduction of block exemption and the reduction in new vehicle margins, more focus is being placed upon the profitability of the Service Department and now that too is under pressure as we are witnessing a wave of change in customer loyalty.

The job role of a Service Manager is also changing. Technical knowledge is a prerequisite, not an outright qualification. The Service Manager of today must know how to make the most out of every opportunity and they need to understand their financial reports in order to gain control. The importance of this area is also evident in the recruitment of senior management. In the past it was *desirable* for a Dealer Principal to have an understanding of the Service Department, now it is deemed to be ***absolutely essential*** to ensure the survival of the dealership.

As the opening quotation states, "*The man who views the world at 50 the same as he did at 20 has wasted 30 years of his life*", surely the message here is that everything is changing and as we grow older we learn more and become wiser. If someone tells you that they have been in the industry for 20 years does that mean they have 20 years experience, or does it mean that they have 1 years experience 20 times over? The difference is the constant desire to be better, regardless of the results. Obviously, you are reading this book because you want to produce better results in your business, but before you get started, I'd like you to spend a few minutes reading a short story that will stimulate your imagination and I'll be making reference to it throughout the book. The story itself has raised several millions in hard cash, so it's certainly worth investing a few minutes here.

ACRES OF DIAMONDS

This story has appeared in many journals and lectures around the world because it is one of those stories that will make you stop and think. "Acres of Diamonds" is a true story that was originally told by Dr Russell H. Conwell in the latter part of the 19th century.

The story is of a farm located next to the River Indus and the owner of the farm was a Persian man named Al Hafed. He was a wealthy and contented man; contented because he was wealthy and wealthy because he was contented.

A Buddhist priest visited Al Hafed at his farm and told him exciting stories about diamonds and their incredible value. The priest told him that if he had a hand full diamonds, Al Hafed would be able to purchase the entire country, and with a mine full of these diamonds he would be able to place all of his children upon the royal thrones of countries throughout the world.

That night, Al Hafed went to bed and could think of nothing else but diamonds and the wealth that they could bring him. He was excited so much by the potential of such wealth that he could not sleep. Now Al Hafed was a poor man, not because he had lost anything, because he hadn't. He was poor because he was discontented and he was discontented because he thought he was poor.

Al Hafed made plans to sell his farm so that he could raise the money to go prospecting for diamonds mines of his own. Within a very short time, he sold his farm, collected his money and left his wife and children in the care of a neighbour until his safe return. He left the farm and headed for the mountains. After fruitless searching, he went prospecting in Palestine and then into Europe. Finally, when his money was all gone, he had still not found a single diamond, and in a fit of despondency and desperation he committed suicide in the Bay of Barcelona.

During this time, the man who bought Al Hafed's farm led his camel out for a drink of water, and when his camel put its head down into the stream next to his farmhouse, he noticed a brilliant flash of light from the sands of the shallow water. He reached in and pulled out a piece of crystal that reflected all the colours of the rainbow. It was not a pretty stone, it had an irregular shape, but nevertheless he took the stone to his home and put it on his fireplace.

Several weeks later, the priest that had told Al Hafed about diamonds came to visit the new owner of the farm. Whilst inside his house, the priest saw the brilliant flashes of light emanating from the piece of crystal that was sitting on the fireplace. He rushed over to pick it up, hefted it in his hand, looked at it closely and he asked the farmer if he knew what he had found. When the farmer said that he thought it was a piece of crystal, the priest became very excited and proclaimed that it was not a crystal that he had found; it was a diamond!

The farmer laughed and told the priest that he must be wrong because the streams on his farm were full of these crystals. The priest then asked the farmer to take him outside to see if he could find more of these sparkling crystals. In a state mixed with disbelief and excitement, they went outside together, and using their fingers they sifted through the shallows of a stream right next to the house. Within a very short time they found more of the beautifully coloured stones, just like the one on the fireplace. However, just as the priest had thought, they were not pieces of crystal, every single one of the irregular shaped, light-emitting stones was a diamond.

The farmer stood up with his right hand full of gems, he looked across the huge expanse of his farm and he took in a deep breath as he realised that he owned acres of diamonds.

The farm that Al Hafed had sold so that he might find a diamond mine, turned out to be the diamond mines of Golconda, the most productive diamond mines on the entire African continent. The great Kohinoor diamond in Britain's crown jewels and the largest crown diamond on earth in Russia's crown jewels came from that mine. Al Hafed had owned acres of diamonds, but he had sold them for practically nothing in order to look for them elsewhere.

The moral of the story is clear: if only Al Hafed had taken the time to prospect and utilise the land he already owned before looking elsewhere, he would have found far more diamonds than he could have possibly imagined. If he had taken the time to learn what diamonds look like in their raw state, his wildest dreams would have come true. The diamonds were there all along; they had always been there, right under his nose. He simply couldn't see them.

This is where you face your own personal challenge. Your Service Department is also full of diamonds, they have always been there, right under your nose, but it takes imagination to see them and you may have to think a little differently or even learn new skills to convert them into business practices that will boost your profits. The real question to ask yourself is this: Do you honestly believe that you have enough desire and determination to rise to this challenge?

To prospect for your own acres of diamonds, continue reading with an open mind and take a fresh look at the ideas presented to you in the following chapters and remember that you may not see the diamonds the first time you look; just don't make the same mistake as Al Hafed.

In the months that follow you will learn to treat this book like one of your favourite paintings; every time you look at it, you will see something new. When this begins to happen you will know that your ability is growing because you are seeing new opportunities around you. Just follow these simple rules that will keep you on the right path to success:

When you are presented with new ideas, or you think of new ideas yourself, don't make an immediate judgement on their value. Some of them may not be applicable to your business today, but things change and the idea may have some value at a later date. Make a habit of flicking through your ideas every few months because one of them may be emitting a bright light that you could not see the first time you looked.

Before you spend any money or go looking at other businesses in search of new wealth, first make the most of what you already possess; you may already be sitting on your own acres of diamonds. Keep in mind that real vision in business comes not from seeking new landscapes, but in having new eyes. Learn to look at your business in different ways and try new ideas.

It was Francis Bacon that first coined the phrase "Knowledge itself is power", but I believe this to be wrong in today's competitive environment. Reading books and attending training courses will give you more knowledge but now I'm giving you a new dimension to think about whilst reading this book:

"Knowledge plus action equals power"

This book will show you where the diamonds are located, but it is up to you to pick them up and take action by doing something with them.

Happy prospecting!

PART I

UNDERSTANDING YOUR OPERATIONAL EFFICIENCIES

Jeff Smith - How to make more profit with your Service Department

CHAPTER I

UNDERSTANDING YOUR UTILISATION

*"People travel to wonder at the height of mountains,
at the huge waves of the seas,
at the long course of the rivers,
at the vast compass of the ocean,
at the circular motion of the stars,
and yet they pass by themselves without wondering."*

- Saint Augustine

Chapter I

Understanding Your Utilisation

Hours Worked ÷ Hours Attended (x100)

Benchmark: 85% to 95%

Let's get straight to the point. Utilisation is without doubt the most powerful profit builder within the whole of the Service Department, yet few people truly understand it, even fewer people calculate it accurately on their management reports and more importantly, even fewer people know how to exploit it to grow their profits. This chapter will explain the full meaning of Utilisation and how to calculate it.

Learning To Look Within

The quotation on the previous page by Saint Augustine suggests that we sometimes overlook what we already have and the greatest treasures are often to be found right under our nose. At some point in your life you will have visited a number of different tourist attractions around the country, but have you visited the attractions in your local area? Most people have not and do not make use of (or utilise) their local attractions.

This same philosophy is also applicable for seeking new business opportunities, and it was made abundantly clear to me when two of my good friends decided to change their jobs. My friend named Simon works in Sales Management within the Motor Industry. He left all his family and friends in his home country of Australia and came to work in Great Britain. When I asked him why he has travelled to the other side of the world to be a Sales Manager he said that it is because of the wonderful opportunities that exist in Sales Management over here.

I have another friend named John, who is also in Sales Management. John has also left all his family and friends in his home country of Great Britain to go to work in Australia. When I asked him why he wanted to travel to the other side of the world to be a Sales Manager, he said it was because of the wonderful opportunities that exist in Sales Management over there.

The moral of the story is clear. We usually see growth and opportunity outside of our immediate field of vision. We will literally travel to the other side of the world in pursuit of new opportunities, yet we fail to see the opportunities that are right under our nose.

Utilisation is the key performance indicator that informs you of whether you are making the most of the resources that are right under your nose in your Service Department. It is by far the most powerful profit builder because when you grow your business from the inside, you are making the most of the resources that you already possess and the increases in profit go directly to your bottom line.

UTILISATION EXPLAINED
Imagine for a moment that you are a General Manager in control of a power station. Your job is to

produce electricity and distribute it to the local area. Most businesses, like a parts department for instance, can keep their products in stock, but as you know, you cannot store electricity. You have to use it immediately, or it's lost.

It is obvious that if you sell 90% of the electricity that you produce you will make more profit than if you only sold 70% because your production costs remain the same. If you only sell 70% of your electricity, that means 30% will be wasted because you cannot store the additional electricity that you have produced.

When you understand this very simple concept, you come to the realisation that <u>time</u> is also like electricity; it cannot be stored and you have to use it immediately, or you lose it.

Utilisation in your workshop is measuring how much of your available time you are using and how much you are wasting. Again it is obvious that if you utilise 90% of your available time you will make more profit than if you only utilise 70% because you still pay your Technicians the same amount of money to turn up for work. If you only utilise 70% of your available time, that means 30% will be wasted because you cannot store your Technicians time.

MEASURING UTILISATION
Utilisation is all about the relationship between Hours Attended and Hours Worked and it measures your ability to convert your Technicians *available* time into *productive* time. There is no point employing Technicians if you are unable to keep them working because that time will be lost. Utilisation is measuring

how well your work is flowing through your workshop and whether your Technicians are being kept busy on jobs that are producing revenue. Any time that is not utilised cannot be stored to use another day and therefore it falls into an expense called Idle Time.

In simplistic terms, a Technician clocks in for 8 hours per day, 5 days per week, but how much of that time has been spent spanner-in-hand, head-under-bonnet working on hours that can be charged to your customers? To keep control over your Utilisation, you need to keep the work flowing through the workshop with as little interruption as possible. Like all areas of performance development, it's easier said than done, but before you get into the detail of how to improve Utilisation, it is useful to know how it is calculated and from where the information is gathered.

The example below demonstrates that the Technicians have attended, and therefore have been *available* to work for 1,226 but only 76% of that time has been utilised.

(A) Hours Worked   = 932
(B) Hours Attended = 1,226
(C) **Utilisation**   = **76%**   (A ÷ B x 100)

Figure 1

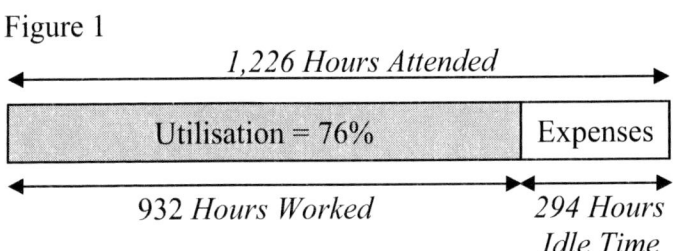

You can see from figure 1 that any attended time that is not spent working productively (or not utilised) is treated as an expense called Idle Time. Therefore, the amount of money that you pay your Technicians to turn up at your business (Hours Attended) is the sum total of the Hours Worked plus Idle Time.

Yes, you still have to pay your Technicians to come to work whether they are working productively or not, so you might ask what is the point of measuring Utilisation? This is a very easy question to answer. What is the point of paying for something that you do not use? Or better still, if you make *more* use of what you already have, you will make more profit.

Utilisation is measuring how well you are using the time that is available to you. Obviously, if you utilise 90% of your time, you will make more profit than if you use only 70% because you cannot store the remaining 30%; it is wasted.

The benchmark for Utilisation is 85% - 95%, which means that 85% is not a good result, but if your Utilisation is any lower than this, your department profitability will be suffering to a great extent. The example in figure 1 on the previous page illustrating Utilisation at 76% would be a disastrous result because that would mean that 24% of the Technicians time would not be utilised; that's a real waste of time!

WHAT ABOUT OVERTIME?
The reason for the payment of overtime is because you have more work going through the workshop than you can cope with during your normal working day. At this point you pay your Technicians more

money to work additional hours so that the extra work can be completed. No great secrets or surprises here, BUT why would you want to pay overtime if your Utilisation is low?

If you are paying overtime and your Utilisation is reporting low, let's say around 80%, profit is leaking out of your department just as water leaks through a colander. You are in effect paying your Technicians to attend and only utilising 80% of their time and with overtime payments, you are paying more money to make up for the fact that 20% of the normal working day has been wasted. This means that your wage bill significantly increases along with your overheads and with so much Idle Time, you would not have the ability to take on additional work, so it's a financial and operational disaster. In all probability, it may be that only 80% of the overtime that you are paying is utilised too!

Overtime payments are all well and good where they are properly justified. When Utilisation is greater than 90%, there will be some occasions where you will need your Technicians to work overtime, but if you pay overtime when Utilisation is low, your costs will be increasing for no good reason.

* * * * *

To conclude this chapter, I'll leave you with this one final thought. You cannot store time, you must use it immediately, or you lose it forever. The danger is that unless you measure Utilisation you cannot *see* time and it gets overlooked and time is often wasted together with your opportunities to make more profit. The easiest and most profitable way to grow your business is to make the most of what you already possess.

CHAPTER II

UNDERSTANDING YOUR PRODUCTIVITY

"When you are in a business where you exchange time for money, you had better get it right because you only get one chance."

- Jeff Smith

Chapter II

Understanding Your Productivity

Hours Sold ÷ Hours Worked Productively (x100)

Benchmark: 110% to 125%

Most people will say they have a good understanding of what Productivity is and what it measures and you will usually hear it summarised as this: "Get your Technicians to work faster and complete the jobs quicker than the book time and you will make more profit."

Whilst summaries such as these contain elements of truth, it is only half of the story, which means that there is much more to be gained from Productivity than simply beating the allocated job times. This chapter will explain the full meaning of Productivity and how to monitor it effectively.

Beating The Clock
Productivity is not unique to the Service Department. Personally, I blame that bright ball of light in the sky called the Sun. As planet Earth revolves around this shinning star, it casts its light and shadows over us and so we are locked into a cycle with predictable precision where day follows night leaving us with a structured pattern called time.

Although we might not like to admit it, mankind is totally obsessed and governed by time, so much so that we've even invented clocks to measure it more accurately, or did we invent clocks to measure our own Productivity?

No matter what task you think of in your everyday life, there's almost always a timescale or a deadline that comes with it. Productivity is measured in most service-based industries, even heart surgery, and in general terms it is the measurement of the ability to complete tasks within an allocated timescale. However, this can sometimes be very dangerous because when you are in a business where you exchange time for money, you had better get it right first time because you only get one chance; time waits for no one.

If the stipulated time for a triple-heart-bypass is eight hours and the Surgeon takes three days to complete the job, the patient will probably die. Thankfully for us, Service Department Productivity is not quite so critical. However, if the Surgeon completes the eight-hour bypass in just two hours, he probably would not receive a time-saved bonus payment either and you probably would not want to be operated on by a Surgeon who gets paid in this way would you?

Most of your customers think the same way about their vehicles too. Productivity bonuses can be very damaging to your overall performance, but more about that subject in later chapters. Essentially, you are operating a business where you are exchanging your Technicians time for your customers money and there is something fundamental to understand about this type of business strategy. Exchanging time for money is a different business to exchanging a product for money because you can build up a stock pile of products and store them, but you can't store time and this type of business brings with it different kinds of pressures. It's not a matter of good *time* management because you cannot manage time. Increasing Productivity is a matter of good *Service* Management either at the front counter to increase the Hours Sold, or in the workshop to decrease the Hours Worked.

PRODUCTIVITY EXPLAINED

Productivity measures the relationship between the number of Hours Sold to your customers and the number of hours that your Technicians are clocked onto their jobs, (Hours Worked) which means that when we look at Productivity in isolation, there are only two areas of influence that produce the result.

Example:
(A) Hours Sold   = 6
(B) Hours Worked = 5
(C) Productivity   = 120.00%   (A ÷ B x 100)

In the example above you can see that the number of Hours Worked are fewer than the number of Hours Sold which means that the Technicians have completed the task in a lesser time than has been charged. However, this does not always happen in real life does it?

Example:
(A) Hours Sold   = 6
(B) Hours Worked = 7
(C) Productivity   = 85.71% (A ÷ B x 100)

In this example you can see that Productivity has fallen below 100%, which means that the Technicians have been working on the job for more time than has been charged. Are these differences in Productivity due to your Technicians, or are they due to Service Management at the front desk? Let's explore this further and discover what factors have an impact upon your performance in this area.

AREAS OF INFLUENCE

Firstly, let's take a closer look at Warranty work and how the Hours Sold are decided. Most manufacturers provide book times for every job that is conducted on every vehicle they build and these book times dictate the number of Hours Sold, or in other words, the book times dictate the number of hours that you are allowed to charge on all Warranty jobs, which means that you have no control over the Hours Sold here.

Although a manufacturer's book times dictate the number of Hours Sold, they do not dictate the number of Hours Worked (the time it takes to complete that job). Now here is a critical point of understanding. Because every warranty job is dictated by a manufacturer's book time in that you are told how many hours you can charge, this means that you can only influence your Productivity with the Hours Worked. This means that when you analyse your Productivity on Warranty work you are really looking at the results of your ability to complete the Warranty work within the dictated book time. It's not just about your Technicians working faster, as you will soon discover there are many things that influence your Productivity.

When you analyse your Productivity on warranty work you will need to be careful because in many cases it is usually lower than 100% because you are not generally given time for the diagnostics; only the time for the repair. Your Technicians will need to spend time on diagnosis and therefore there is a tendency for your Technicians to work more hours on the job than can be charged. It is also quite difficult to benchmark Productivity on warranty work simply because some manufacturers are more generous than others with their book times.

Explaining Productivity on warranty work in this manner clearly demonstrates that the number of Hours Sold is dictated by the manufacturer and any increase in performance can only be achieved by decreasing the number of Hours Worked.

In summary then, if your Technicians are able to complete their jobs in fewer hours than have been sold your Productivity increases. If they take longer to complete their jobs than has been sold then your Productivity decreases.

GAINING MORE CONTROL

Whilst it is true that manufacturer book time dictate the number of Hours Sold for Warranty work, it is not true for all other types of work such as Retail and Internal. Manufacturer book times in these areas are generally used as guidance rather than an absolute dictate which means that the Hours Sold can often deviate from the manufacturer book times. In these instances it is up to the Service Manager and the Service Receptionist to decide how many hours are to be charged to your customer and therefore the control of the Hours Sold is taken out of the hands of the manufacturer and placed into your hands. Also remember that you are also still in control of the number of Hours Worked.

The general idea of Productivity is that your Hours Sold should be higher than your Hours Worked. The number of Hours Sold is decided by the customer-facing staff and the number of Hours Worked is decided by the Technicians and both are controlled by the Service Manger. Naturally you will want to know how to influence each of these areas and that information is covered in Chapter VI.

DOES TIME REALLY EQUAL MONEY?
Here is a short story that shows a very good example of how Productivity influences your profitability. It's a story that has been told many times by many different people and it demonstrates the point very well.

At the end of the nineteenth century, a Mill Owner in the North of England was beside himself with worry. The steam boiler that provided light and power throughout his entire factory had broken down. Many experts had attempted to repair it, but none had been successful. "Time is money," he kept repeating to himself as he counted the cost of lost production. "Time is money."

After several days of sheer desperation, a man in blue overalls was shown into the Mill Owners office. "I understand that you have a problem with your boiler, and I believe that I can fix it for you" he said.

The Mill Owner was unimpressed. "I've had the best people there are in the industry trying to repair the boiler and they have all failed. Look at you. You've only got one small tool bag and not much in it if I'm not mistaken."

"Well Sir, that is correct, but for this job I only need the specific tools necessary for this particular predicament. I can see that you are not yet convinced so would you like me to leave or would you prefer me to have a quick look at your boiler while I'm here?"

Still unimpressed, but thinking he had nothing to lose, the Mill Owner led the man in blue overalls to the boiler room where the broken boiler was located. Emanating from it were miles and miles of piping, snaking towards every corner of the factory.

The boiler room was filled with the sounds of knocking, clunking, and hissing from the large network of pipes and valves, but it was the absence of the noise of the machinery in the mill that was most deafening.

In a somewhat patronising tone the Mill Owner invited the man to have a quick look at the boiler to see if he could fix it.

Quietly and without any fuss, the man in the blue overalls selected one tool from his tool bag; it was a very small metal hammer, the kind of hammer that you use to break toffee.
Delicately and methodically, he began to tap gently in various places, listening carefully to the responses he obtained. For ten minutes he tapped at pressure

valves, thermostats, u-bends, collars and joints where he thought that problems might exist. Finally, he returned to his tool bag and replaced his small metal hammer and selected and much larger wooden mallet. He stepped up to a complex elbow at one section of piping and gave it a firm and powerful thump with the mallet. The effect was instantaneous. As if a large blockage had been shifted, water began to flow, steam began to pump and a loud cheer was heard from the workers in the factory as the machines in the mill burst into life once again.

The Mill Owner was absolutely delighted and in a state of pure excitement and relief, he thrust his arms into the air and said, "Marvellous, marvellous, you have saved my business, well done! Send me the bill and double your normal price."

The man in the blue overalls said "Thank you very much for your generosity sir, but that will not be necessary. I will send you a bill for my usual fee." He packed his wooden mallet away into his tool bag and left the Mill when he was satisfied that the blockage had completely cleared.

When the bill arrived some days later, the Mill Owner was stunned because the amount was far more than he had expected. The invoice was for £100 sterling; a huge sum of money for those days.

Although he had paid £100 to some of the other companies who had failed to fix the problem, they had been there for days, and the man in the blue overalls had been there for only ten minutes.

The Mill Owner instructed his secretary to send a letter asking for a breakdown of these costs. How can he justify charging £100 for just 10 minutes of his time?

The man in the blue overalls reformatted his invoice and sent his reply by post which read as follows:

Invoice	
For ten minutes of diagnosis and tapping to identify the problem	£1
For knowing where to tap and fixing the problem	£99
Total Payable	**£100**

The moral of the story is clear. When you know what you are doing, you can complete a task in far less time than otherwise expected whilst still charging the same amount of money as everyone else and the result is a higher Gross Profit on that particular job. When you have the right tools for the job and you know how to use them time does not equal money, but expertise certainly does. Remember that it is both technical expertise and management expertise that produces the increase in your results.

If the man in the blue overalls had spent the whole day at the Mill, then his cost of sales (his time) would have been much higher. However, because he only spent ten minutes at the Mill, he had the rest of the day left free for him to get something else done.

Of course the real secret to success is making sure that you have something else to do for the rest of the day, otherwise all that you achieve is a huge amount of Idle Time and that just increases your Expenses.

MEASURING PRODUCTIVITY

To measure productivity effectively, you need to have your Technicians clocking on and off each job so that you can accurately identify how much time has been spent spanner-in-hand, head-under-bonnet working on each job. If your Technicians do not use the clock effectively, you will not know the number of Hours Worked, you will be blind to any shortfalls in this area of operational performance and you could be led into making wrong decisions about your Service Department.

In addition to this, some Technicians are quicker than others, and some Technicians have skills that others do not possess and therefore it is wise to measure the Productivity of the department as a whole and also to measure each Technicians performance individually so that you can clearly see where your strengths and weaknesses lie. Most financial reports capture the total Hours Sold and the total Hours Worked so that you can see your departmental performance, but they will not show each individual Technicians performance. This is relatively easy for you to capture on a weekly report and if you require some guidance in this area, you can download a sample report format to get you started from the Insight web site at www.AskInsight.com/service96

BENCHMARKING PRODUCTIVITY

The benchmarks for Productivity are a lower limit of 110% and an upper limit of 125%. This 15% tolerance between the figures is to account for the varying skills of your Technicians and the type and mix of work that you are undertaking. If your workload consists mainly of scheduled servicing, then your Productivity should be high, but if your workload consists of mainly repair work or warranty work, then your Productivity may be lower and let's not forget the selling abilities of your customer-facing staff.

* * * * *

To conclude this chapter, I'll leave you with this one final thought. Don't get caught up in the mistaken belief that beating the allocated job times alone is the saviour of the Service Department; it is not.

Beating the allocated job times is a great profit builder, but it does not get more work flowing through the workshop, it merely creates the "opportunity" to get more work through the workshop by completing jobs quicker and thereby releasing more free time to complete another job. If you do not fill the extra time that you have created with another job, you will lose the advantage that you have gained. The most profitable way to increase your Productivity is to increase the number of Hours Sold and that is the task of the customer-facing people on the front desk.

CHAPTER III

UNDERSTANDING YOUR OVERALL EFFICIENCY

*"For every action,
there is an opposite and equal reaction."*

- Sir Isaac Newton

Chapter III

Understanding Your Overall Efficiency

The secret to increasing your profitability lies within your ability to control your work, rather than your work controlling you. This chapter explains how Overall Efficiency measures the performance of the Service Department enabling you to control the direction of your business.

Overall Efficiency Explained

The basic calculation for Overall Efficiency is Hours Sold divided by Hours Attended and the general idea to succeed in business is that you need to sell more hours than your Technicians attend. It's not rocket science, it's pocket science. When Hours Sold are greater than Hours Attended, Overall Efficiency will be reporting greater than 100%.

This being said, it's critically important to understand that you do not have any *direct* control over your Overall Efficiency because it is only a result that is generated from other areas of your performance. You cannot do anything at an operational level to improve your Overall Efficiency because the Hours Sold are controlled by Productivity and the Hours Attended are controlled by Utilisation. Therefore if you wish to improve your Overall Efficiency you have to achieve it by improving your Productivity and Utilisation.

Understanding that Overall Efficiency is the product of your Productivity and Utilisation is fundamental to gaining control of your Service Department because it informs you whether all your hard work and efforts are achieving harmony and balance on the shop floor. Let's take a closer look at how the three operational efficiencies work together.

There are three inextricable links that exists between all three of the operational efficiencies of the Service Department and understanding these links unlock the secrets of how to operate the department more effectively, and also how to make more profit but remember that a chain is only as strong as it weakest link so you really need a good understanding of how these links operate.

You already know that the basic formula for Overall Efficiency is Hours Sold ÷ Hours Attended x 100 but there is also another method of calculating Overall Efficiency which is much more revealing about the skills of the management team. The formula is:

Utilisation x Productivity = Overall Efficiency

It doesn't matter whether you use this formula or Hours Sold ÷ Hours Attended because the answer you will get is exactly the same. However, it is the understanding of the fact that Overall Efficiency is the result of Utilisation *multiplied by* Productivity that yields the real power. This point is critical because it means that you must increase your Productivity by getting your Technicians to beat the allocated job times *and you must also* increase your Utilisation by filling the time you have saved with more work otherwise there's no point in beating the allocated job times because you will just create Idle Time.

OPPOSITE AND EQUAL REACTIONS

Sir Isaac Newton taught us that for every action, there is an opposite and equal reaction. Within the Service Department this effect is evident between Productivity and Utilisation because they are constantly pushing and pulling against each other to gain dominance. Let's take a closer look at how this happens on the shop floor by building a simple business model so that the effects of any performance development can be clearly seen. The following examples demonstrate how Newton's law of opposite and equal reactions affect your operational performance and why it is so important to monitor your Overall Efficiency.

THE BASIC MODEL

(A) Number of Technicians = 4
(B) Hours Attended p/Tech. = 40
(C) Total Hours Attended = 160   (A x B)

Now let's make it nice and easy and say that the Hours Worked are reported at 144 and the Hours Sold are reported at 158.40 which means that the three Operational Efficiencies can now be calculated:

(D) Hours Worked   = 144
(E) Hours Sold   = 158.40
(F) **Utilisation**   = 90%   (D ÷ C x 100)
(G) **Productivity**   = 110% (E ÷ D x 100)
(H) **Overall Efficiency** = 99%   (E ÷ C x 100)

By using this model you will see what happens to the operational performance in the Service Department when something changes and how it is then reported in your operational efficiencies.

Understanding Your Overall Efficiency

In this next example, let's say that the department successfully increases Productivity to 120% by the Technicians completing their work quicker than the allocated job times, but the questions are:

1. What will happen to the operational performance of the department?

2. What will happen to the Overall Efficiency?

The model below provides the gain in Productivity and the asterisk marks show the figures that will need to be recalculated in order to illustrate the changes in operational performance. Obviously, the question mark remains on Overall Efficiency.

(A) Number of Technicians = 4
(B) Hours Attended p/Tech. = 40
(C) Total Hours Attended = 160
(D) Hours Worked = *
(E) Hours Sold = 158.40
(F) Utilisation = *
(G) Productivity = 120%
(H) Overall Efficiency = ?

STAGE 1: GETTING STARTED
The department has increased Productivity to 120% by the Technicians beating the allocated job times which means that they spend less time clocked onto each job and the result is that the Hours Worked will be reduced. In order to obtain the revised number of Hours Worked, you take the Hours Sold and divide it by the new Productivity figure of 120% as you can see highlighted in bold on the following page.

(A) Number of Technicians = 4
(B) Hours Attended p/Tech. = 40
(C) Total Hours Attended = 160
(D) Hours Worked = 132 (E ÷ G x 100)
(E) Hours Sold = 158.40
(F) Utilisation = *
(G) Productivity = 120%
(H) Overall Efficiency = ?

STAGE 2: RECALCULATE UTILISATION

Now that the Hours Worked are in place it's possible to calculate the changes that have taken place within Utilisation. The formula for Utilisation is Hours Worked divided by Hours Attended. You can see how this is calculated from the example below.

(A) Number of Technicians = 4
(B) Hours Attended p/Tech. = 40
(C) Total Hours Attended = 160
(D) Hours Worked = 132
(E) Hours Sold = 158.40
(F) Utilisation = 82.5% (D ÷ C x 100)
(G) Productivity = 120%
(H) Overall Efficiency = ?

STAGE 3: RECALCULATE OVERALL EFFICIENCY

You recall that the object of this exercise is to understand what happens to Overall Efficiency when Productivity is increased by beating the allocated job times.

The formula for Overall Efficiency is Utilisation multiplied by Productivity therefore when you take the figures from the model above the answer to the question is 82.5 x 120 ÷ 100 = 99%.

LOT'S OF PAIN, BUT NO GAIN!
The model shows an increase in Productivity by beating the allocated job times and most people expect to see an increase in operational performance here, but Overall Efficiency has remained constant at 99% so *why* has the department not made any improvement?

The reason for this seemingly odd result is because the Hours Worked are reduced in the exercise to improve Productivity but the Hours Worked are common to both Productivity and Utilisation.

When you increase Productivity in this way you *automatically* decrease Utilisation and it is the multiplication of these two areas that deliver Overall Efficiency. It's rather like a seesaw. As one goes up, the other goes down and the point in the middle remains constant. In the exercise, Productivity went up to 120% but Utilisation went down to 82.5% and Overall Efficiency (the point in the middle) remains constant. This exercise confirms that there is no reward gained from focussing all your attention on either Utilisation or Productivity, you must focus your attention upon both of these areas if you are to realise any improvement in operational performance.

SLIDING SCALES
Utilisation and Productivity are like Siamese twins; you can't talk about one without talking about the other. To demonstrate this let's take a more advanced and more graphic look at how and why Utilisation and Productivity are so inseparable and how they affect your operational performance and Overall Efficiency.

Consider the three slide controls below to represent the numbers of hours in each sector of the exercise you have just completed. As you move the slide controls to the left the numbers of hours reduce and when you move the slide control to the right the numbers of hours increase. Below the slide controls you can see that the three operational efficiencies have been calculated.

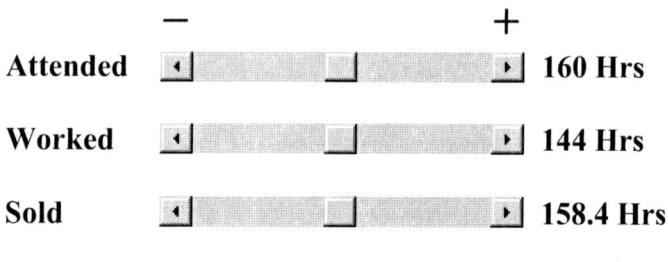

Attended — ◀ ▬▬▬▬ ▶ **160 Hrs**

Worked ◀ ▬▬▬▬ ▶ **144 Hrs**

Sold ◀ ▬▬▬▬ ▶ **158.4 Hrs**

Productivity = 110% (Sold ÷ Worked)
Utilisation = 90% (Worked ÷ Attended)
Overall Efficiency = 99% (Sold ÷ Attended)

The first part of the exercise saw the Productivity increase to 120% by the Technicians beating the allocated jobs times and therefore reducing the Hours Worked. Now look at the slide controls in this next illustration to see the effects of this action.

Attended ◀ ▬▬▬▬ ▶ **160 Hrs**

Worked ◀ ▬▬▬▬ ▶ **132 Hrs**

Sold ◀ ▬▬▬▬ ▶ **158.4 Hrs**

You can see from this example that the number of Hours Worked reduced to facilitate the gain in Productivity, but this action *automatically* reduced Utilisation because the Hours Worked are common to both.

Productivity   = 120%   (Increased)
Utilisation   = 82.5%   (Decreased)
Overall Efficiency = 99%   (Constant)

This point is critical to understand because when you attempt to improve Productivity or Utilisation by affecting the number of Hours Worked, you must understand that you will encounter an opposite and equal reaction. In other words, when you increase one, you *automatically* decrease the other.

The reason that there was no improvement in the operational performance in the exercise is because the increase in Productivity *automatically* caused a decrease in Utilisation and the end result is the same.

At this stage the slide control for the number of Hours Worked can be recalibrated and relabelled to illustrate the effect that it has upon your operational efficiencies.

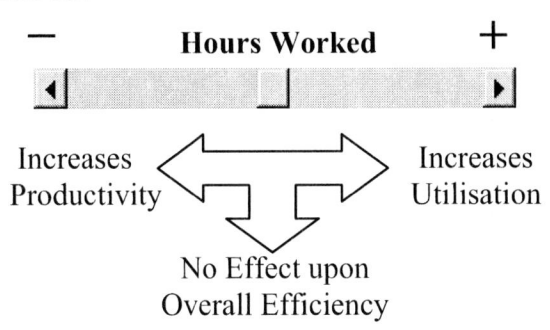

—   **Hours Worked**   +

Increases Productivity   ⇔   Increases Utilisation

No Effect upon Overall Efficiency

THE SECRETS OF SUCCESS

When you want to increase the Overall Efficiency of the Service Department you have to improve both Productivity and Utilisation at the same time. In other words, you need to get your Technicians to beat the allocated job times and at the same time increase your Utilisation by feeding more work into the time that you have saved thereby increase the volume of work and increasing the Hours Sold.

When you increase your Productivity by beating the allocated job times all that you are doing is creating the *opportunity* to make more profit. If you fail to get more work into the time that you have saved, then all of your efforts will have been in vein.

Now let's take another look at the exercise and consider how the slide controls move when you are successful at improving Productivity and Utilisation at the same time.

STAGE 1: PRIOR TO ANY CHANGE

Attended   160 Hrs

Worked   144 Hrs

Sold   158.4 Hrs

	Stage 1	2	3
Productivity	110%		
Utilisation	90%		
Overall Efficiency	99%		

STAGE 2: INCREASE IN PRODUCTIVITY

Productivity was increased to 120% by beating the allocated job times and the Hours Worked reduced together with Utilisation as a direct result of this action, as you can see from the slide controls and the table below.

	− +	
Attended	◄ ▬▬▬▬▬▬▬▬▬ ►	160 Hrs
Worked	◄ ▬▬▬▬▬▬▬▬▬ ►	132 Hrs
Sold	◄ ▬▬▬▬▬▬▬▬▬ ►	158.4 Hrs

	Stage		
	1	2	3
Productivity	110%	120%	
Utilisation	90%	82.5%	
Overall Efficiency	99%	99%	

STAGE 3: INCREASE IN UTILISATION

This is the part that most managers overlook. The Hours Worked have reduced which means that Idle Time has increased and so the skill of the management team now is to increase the Utilisation by putting more jobs through the workshop in the time that has been saved.

When you increase the volume of jobs through the workshop not only do you increase the number of Hours Worked, you also increase the number of Hours Sold and it is this that is the key to success to making more profit.

Increasing Productivity by beating the allocated job times does not increase the Hours Sold, it is Utilisation that does that job and it is your Overall Efficiency that tells you whether you are achieving the balance between these two on the shop floor.

When Utilisation is increased up to 95% whilst Productivity remains at the already improved figure of 120% it is at this time when you improve your operational performance. Here is what you do:

CALCULATING THE GAINS

Utilisation has increased up to 95% due to more jobs being put through therefore the Hours Worked will increase. Hours Attended have remained constant at 160 Hours and Utilisation says that 95% of that time has been spent working on jobs. To recalculate the revised number of Hours Worked you simply take the 160 Hours Attended and multiply them by the value of Utilisation, which in this case is 95%. Therefore 160 x 95% = 152 Hours Worked.

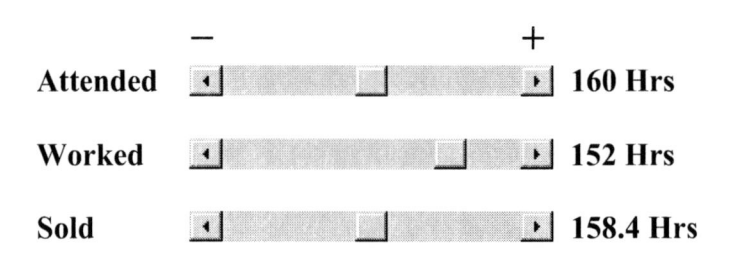

	−	+	
Attended			160 Hrs
Worked			152 Hrs
Sold			158.4 Hrs

Now we can apply the gain in Productivity and see the improvement in operational performance. The Technicians have been working spanner-in-hand clocked onto jobs for 152 hours and their rate of Productivity is now running at 120% therefore the revised number of Hours Sold can be recalculated as follows. You simply take the number of Hours Worked and multiply that by the rate of Productivity, which in this case is 120%. Therefore the calculation is 152 x 120% = 182.4 Hours Sold. You can see how this increase has been applied to the slide controls and the table below.

Attended   160 Hrs

Worked   152 Hrs

Sold   182.4 Hrs

	Stage 1	Stage 2	Stage 3
Productivity	110%	120%	120%
Utilisation	90%	82.5%	95%
Overall Efficiency	99%	99%	114%

You can now see from stage 2 in the table above that when you increase your Productivity by beating the allocated job times, there is no gain in Overall Efficiency because the reduction in the Hours Worked *automatically* reduces your Utilisation.

In stage 3, you can see that it is the management team's ability to increase Utilisation when the Technicians are beating the allocated job times that improves Overall Efficiency.

The only way to increase your Overall Efficiency and ultimately your profitability is to maintain balance between your Utilisation and Productivity. This means that your Technicians need to clock on and off jobs correctly so that you can accurately optimise Utilisation by getting more work through the workshop *and at the same time* get that work done in a quicker time than is allocated because it is the multiplication of these two factors that delivers more profit to your bottom line.

Some managers believe that increasing Productivity by beating the allocated job times is the road to success and you can see from this chapter that this is not true. Beating the allocated job times provides you a higher Labour Gross Profit on *that* particular job, but it does not deliver any more profit to the bottom line because it gets eaten up by the expense called Idle Time. You can improve your Productivity by increasing the Hours Sold, but as you will discover later in the book, that is the job of the front counter staff, not the Technicians.

* * * * *

To conclude this chapter I'll leave you with a final thought. The best Service Managers in the industry are not good at doing one thing, they are good at keeping everything in balance.

CHAPTER IV

THE LAW OF
THE SERVICE DEPARTMENT

"Everything should be made as simple as possible but not simpler."

- Albert Einstein

Chapter IV

The Law Of The Service Department

Everything that happens in the world is governed by some kind of law. For every action there is an opposite and equal reaction, for every cause, there is an effect, for every beginning there is an end. In this chapter you will discover the law of the Service Department and how it influences your business.

In the previous three chapters each key performance indicator has been isolated so that you can see how each of them affects your operational performance on an individual basis.

Whilst it is essential to know how each key performance indicator influences your business, where the information comes from and how to calculate them, it is also essential to know how they work in conjunction with each other, but before you read on here is a reminder of the basic formulas that have been covered.

Utilisation = Worked ÷ Attended x 100
Benchmark 85% to 95%

Productivity = Sold ÷ Worked x 100
Benchmark 110% to 125%

Overall Efficiency = Sold ÷ Attended x 100
Benchmark to be covered in this chapter

This triangular diagram is an illustration of how your Service Department operates in its most simplistic form. Within each sector of the triangle you can see each key performance indictor together with its formula for calculation (remember to x 100 to attain the percentage). However, it is the placement of the key performance indicators within the triangle that is most significant.

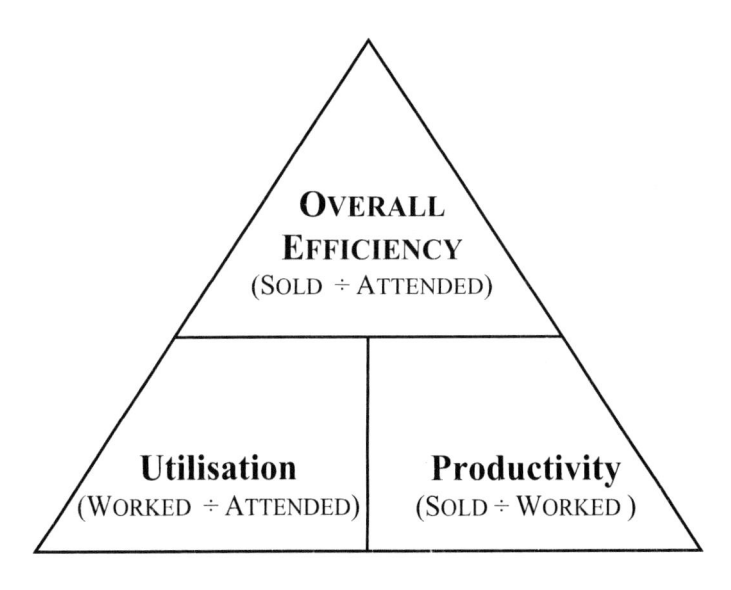

```
                    /\
                   /  \
                  /    \
                 / OVERALL \
                / EFFICIENCY \
               / (SOLD ÷ ATTENDED) \
              /─────────┬─────────\
             / Utilisation │ Productivity \
            /(WORKED ÷ ATTENDED)│(SOLD ÷ WORKED)\
           /_____|_____\
```

You might think that Overall Efficiency is placed at the top of the triangle because it is arguably the most important of the three key performance indicators to measure with Utilisation and Productivity, the working foot soldiers, shown at the bottom of the triangle. In fact, these are not the reasons for their placement in the triangle, but if you keep these thoughts in mind they will help you to remember how the triangle is drawn when you wish to recall this information to mind.

To understand how the law of the Service Department operates you will be using a few models so let's draw an abbreviated model of the law of the Service Department that is more practical for illustration purposes. Here you can see that the full names of the key performance indicators have been abbreviated as follows:

OE = **Overall Efficiency**
U = **Utilisation**
P = **Productivity**

To understand how to use this law, firstly, let's begin by looking at the left-hand side of the triangle. As you can see, Overall Efficiency is on the top of Utilisation with Productivity to the right. Quite simply then, when you write the symbols down and retain the placement as a mathematical formula you would have the following equation: OE over U = P.

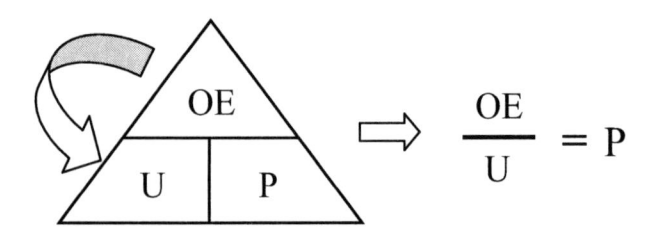

$$\frac{OE}{U} = P$$

This basic equation suggests that Overall Efficiency divided by Utilisation equals Productivity.

To further understand how this works, let's redraw the triangle again, but his time with some figures to replace the symbols representing the key performance indicators.

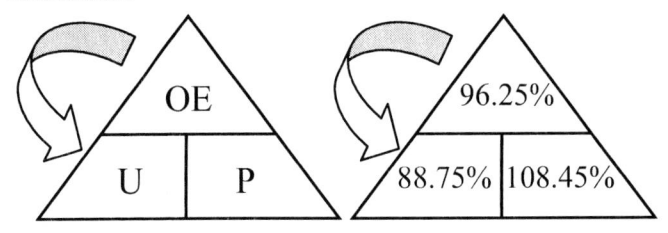

The left-hand triangle will remain in place as a reminder throughout the exercise and the right-hand triangle holds the results relating to each key performance indicator. For instance, the right-hand triangle is stating that Overall Efficiency = 96.25%, Utilisation = 88.75% and Productivity = 108.45%.

Now that we have some figures in place, let's redraw the equation to test the validity of the triangle.

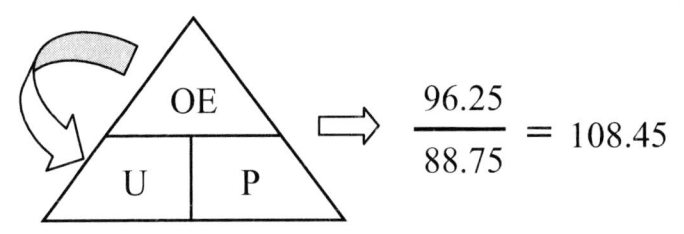

$$\frac{96.25}{88.75} = 108.45$$

Remember that you are dealing with percentages so you will need to multiply by 100 to return your result. Example: 96.25 ÷ 88.75 x100 = 108.45

This example confirms that when you divide your Overall Efficiency by your Utilisation the net result is your Productivity.

Because this formula is true for the left-hand side of the triangle, it is interesting to see that it is also true for the right-hand side of the triangle. Try the maths yourself in this example..

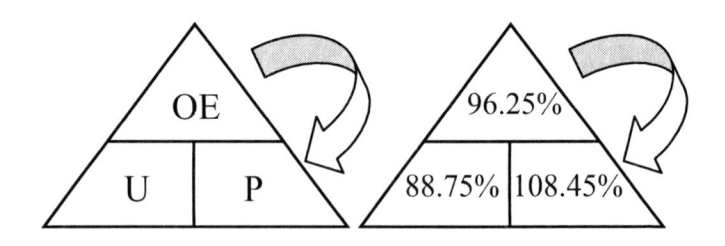

Left-Hand Triangle
Overall Efficiency ÷ Productivity = Utilisation

Right-Hand Triangle
96.25 ÷ 108.45 (x 100) = 88.75%

This illustration also confirms that when you take the figure for your Overall Efficiency and divide it by your Productivity the net result will be your Utilisation. Both of these examples are useful for validating the information that you have gathered because they demonstrate that each key performance indicator is dependent upon the others and if you have any information missing from your figures, now you know how to calculate the missing statistics.

Question: If Overall Efficiency is reported at 93% and Productivity is reported at 123% what is Utilisation? (Try working it out for yourself before you read the answer on the next page.)

Answer: When you use this law you can see that Overall Efficiency ÷ Productivity = Utilisation therefore the answer to the question is calculated as follows: 93 ÷ 123 x 100 = 75.61%.

Now let's complete the exercise by looking at the third and most powerful aspect of the law of the Service Department. You already know from Chapter III that there are two methods for calculating your Overall Efficiency. From your financial reports you might use Hours Sold divided by Hours Attended, but you will recall that you have no direct control over this factor because it is the net result of your Utilisation multiplied by your Productivity. Now let's use the law of the Service Department to illustrate this fact.

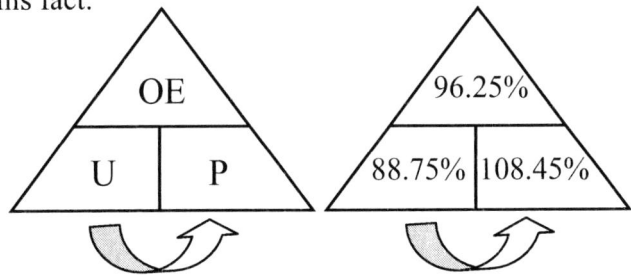

Left-Hand Triangle
Utilisation x Productivity = Overall Efficiency

Right-Hand Triangle
88.75 x 108.45 (÷ 100) = 96.25%

Now that you have all of the rules in place you can use the law of the Service Department model for validating your performance and it is particularly useful in the construction of budgets, business plans and now you can very easily and accurately forecast your operational performance in just a few seconds.

THE LAW OF THE SERVICE DEPARTMENT IN FULL VIEW

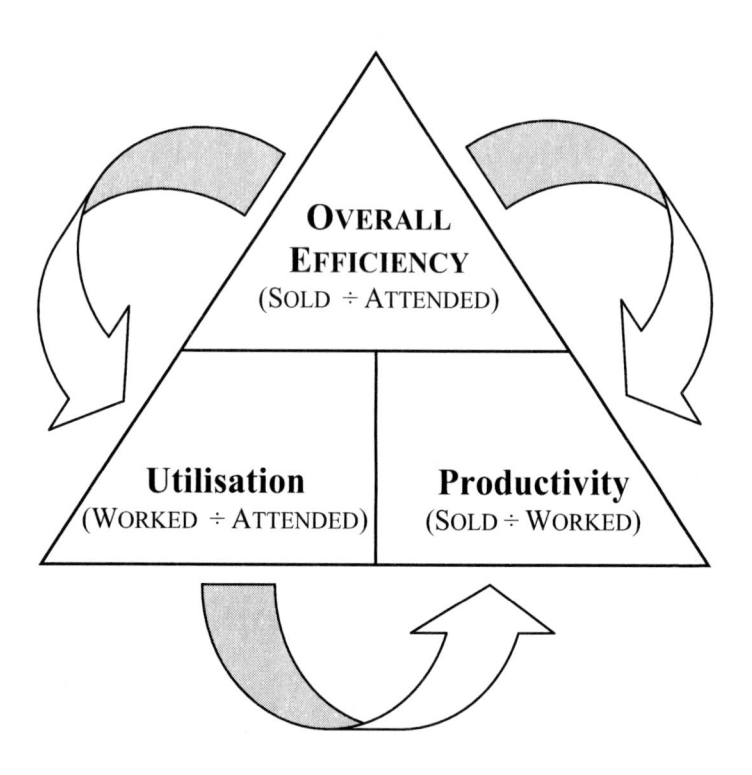

OVERALL EFFICIENCY
(SOLD ÷ ATTENDED)

Utilisation
(WORKED ÷ ATTENDED)

Productivity
(SOLD ÷ WORKED)

Overall Efficiency ÷ Utilisation x 100 = Productivity
Overall Efficiency ÷ Productivity x 100 = Utilisation
Utilisation x Productivity ÷ 100 = Overall Efficiency

You can download and print a full size image of the Law of The Service Department from the Insight website at www.AskInsight.com/service96

UNDERSTANDING CHANGE

Now you know exactly how the law of the Service Department operates, you can use this model to identify how and where you operational performance is changing. The relationship between these key performance indicators is always evident no matter what your figures are reporting. Each area of performance is totally dependant upon the other two areas and therefore the links are inextricable. To demonstrate this fact here is a simple exercise that shows what happens when change happens.

STAGE 1

In this model you have the figures within the triangle and also the slide controls so that you can see the effects of each change as the exercise progresses.

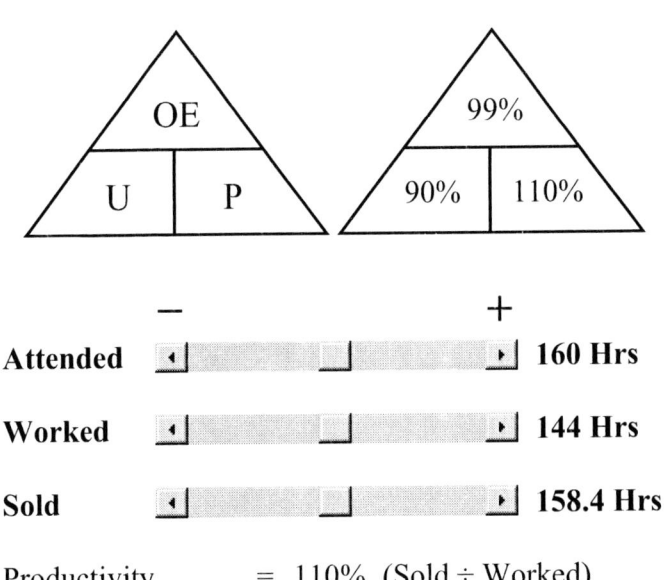

	−	+
Attended		▶ 160 Hrs
Worked		▶ 144 Hrs
Sold		▶ 158.4 Hrs

Productivity   = 110%   (Sold ÷ Worked)
Utilisation   = 90%   (Worked ÷ Attended)
Overall Efficiency = 99%   (Sold ÷ Attended)

Stage 2

Now that the departmental model is in place, it's time to understand what happens to the triangle and the slide controls when there is a change in operational performance. At the moment the slide controls are evenly balanced, but what will happen when Productivity is increased to 120.31% by completing the jobs quicker than the allocated times?

When your Technicians beat the allocated job times the number of Hours Worked reduce and you will see an increase in Productivity. In this case, Productivity has increased to 120% with the Hours Sold remaining at 158.4 therefore the Hours Worked are revised to 132 hours.

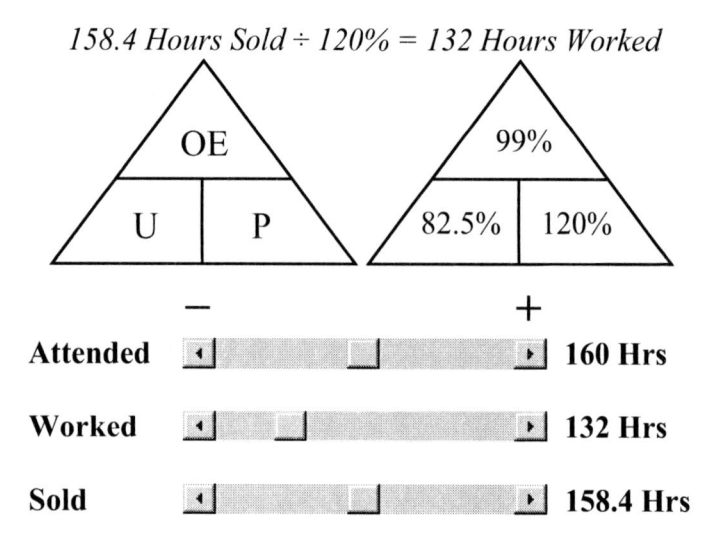

158.4 Hours Sold ÷ 120% = 132 Hours Worked

Attended	—	160 Hrs
Worked		132 Hrs
Sold	+	158.4 Hrs

Here you can see that the Hours Worked is common to both Productivity and Utilisation and therefore as Productivity goes up Utilisation goes down and there is no change in Overall Efficiency.

STAGE 3

Now let's reset Productivity back to its original position of 110% and take a look at what happens when the Technicians do not clock on and off their jobs correctly, which means that the number Hours Worked will increase and therefore there will be an improvement in Utilisation. For the purpose of this example, let's increase Utilisation to 95%.

(Hours Worked = Hours Attended x Utilisation)
(Hours Sold = Hours Worked x Productivity)

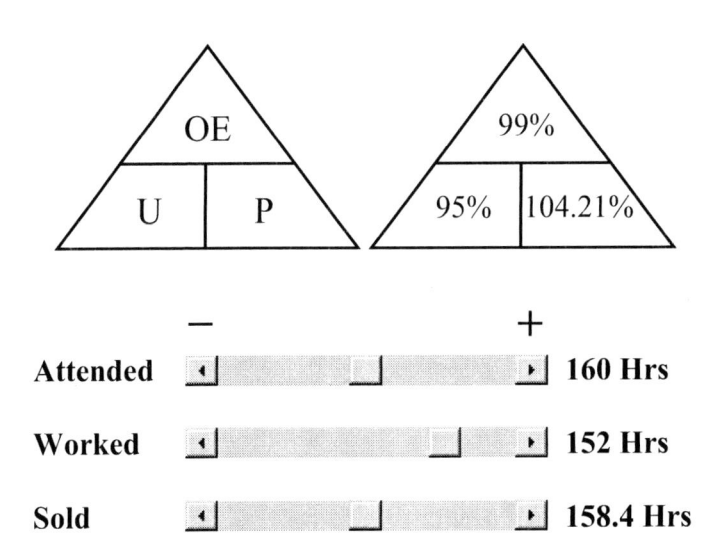

	−		+	
Attended	◄		►	160 Hrs
Worked	◄		►	152 Hrs
Sold	◄		►	158.4 Hrs

Triangles: OE / U / P and 99% / 95% / 104.21%

Here again you can see that the Hours Worked is common to both Productivity and Utilisation and the triangle clearly illustrates that as Utilisation goes up Productivity goes down and there is no change in Overall Efficiency because there has only been focus in one area of operational performance.

STAGE 4

Now let's see what happens when you improve Productivity by beating the allocated job times <u>and</u> also increase your Utilisation by putting more work in to the free time that you have created by beating the job times. In other words, what happens to your operational performance when you maintain balance between Utilisation and Productivity?

In the Stage 2, the Utilisation had fallen to 82.5%, which is a poor result. Now let's increase the Utilisation up to 95% while maintaining Productivity at the higher level 120% that was achieved in Stage 2.

(Hours Worked = Hours Attended x Utilisation)
(Hours Sold = Hours Worked x Productivity)

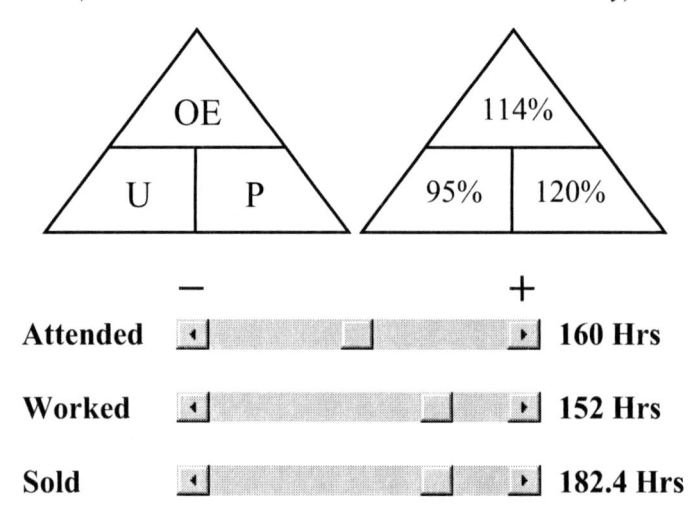

Triangle 1: OE / U | P
Triangle 2: 114% / 95% | 120%

—   +

Attended   160 Hrs

Worked   152 Hrs

Sold   182.4 Hrs

Now you can see the true power of the law of the Service Department because you can forecast your performance with ease and know that it is valid by applying the principles within this simple triangle.

BENCHMARKING OVERALL EFFICIENCY

Now you can use the law of the Service Department to establish the benchmarks for Overall Efficiency.

Utilisation and Productivity are fully explained in their relevant chapters, but for the purpose of this exercise let's say that the benchmark for Utilisation is 85% to 95% and the benchmark for Productivity is 110% to 125%.

Now that you have some figures to work with, you can establish the benchmark levels for Overall Efficiency. In the example below, the left-hand triangle contains the lower limits of the benchmarks for Utilisation and Productivity and the right-hand triangle contains the upper limits. Using this information, the upper and lower benchmarks for Overall Efficiency can be determined as shown.

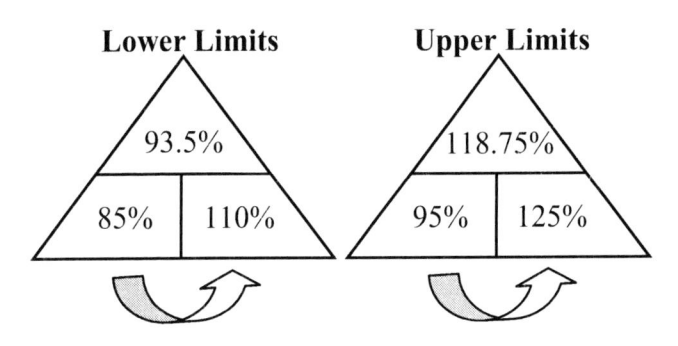

Lower Limits   **Upper Limits**

93.5%   118.75%

85%   110%   95%   125%

Utilisation x Productivity = Overall Efficiency

Left-Hand Triangle
85 x 110 (÷100) = 93.5%

Right-Hand Triangle
95 x 125 (÷100) = 118.75%

You can see from these models that the benchmark for Overall Efficiency is therefore 93.5% to 118.75%. However, these are of course decided by the figures that you insert for your desired results with Utilisation and Productivity.

BRINGING IT ALL TOGETHER
Throughout this chapter you have seen that there are inextricable links between the three main operational efficiencies of your Service Department. Utilisation and Productivity are the foot soldiers that deliver the results to your Overall Efficiency and you must feed them equally to gain the results that you require. There is no point in focussing all of your attention on Productivity if you are unable to fill the time you have gained with another job. Therefore you must focus your attention equally on both Utilisation and Productivity if you are to make any gains in your profitability. The route to success with your Service Department is to keep your Technicians working faster than the allocated job times and filling the time you have gained with additional work and the law of the Service Department will show whether you are achieving this balance or not.

To achieve any modicum of success with your Service Department you need to have your Overall Efficiency reporting greater than 100% and fully understand the trend that it is displaying. If you plot a graph for your Overall Efficiency and it shows very few peaks and troughs, it means that you are focussing your attention on either Utilisation or Productivity and not working on both. Place your figures in to the triangle and you will clearly the strengths and weaknesses of your department.

To conclude this chapter, I'll leave you with this one final thought. The law of the Service Department is constant and the links are inextricable. Use this law to plot your road to success and to balance your skills in the Service Department before you focus all of your effort into making change happen in one given area. This law shows you exactly where your strengths and weaknesses lie and you will need to measure your business activity in this way at least once every month so that you can focus your attention in the right place at the right time and with the right people to maximise your profitability. It's not what you do once in a while that makes a difference; it's what you do on a consistent basis.

*"There's plenty of room at the top
but no where to sit down"*

Part II

How To Improve Your Operational Efficiencies

CHAPTER IV

HOW TO IMPROVE YOUR UTILISATION

*"The real secret of business growth is
not to look for 1 big action that will
grow your business by 100%*

*It is to look for 100 little actions,
each of which will grow your business by 1%."*

- Unknown

Chapter V

How To Improve Your Utilisation

Utilisation is all about the relationship between the Hours Attended (hours clocked in at your business) and the Hours Worked (hours clocked onto jobs). In truth, with the exception of overtime, there's not much that you can do about the Hours Attended except for adding or reducing the number of Technicians that you employ, and reducing the number of Technicians you have is probably one of the last things that you want to do. Therefore all of the ideas contained within this chapter are based upon increasing the number of Hours Worked so that you can get more jobs flowing through your normal working day because when this happens you will increase the number of Hours Sold and these new-found profits will be delivered straight to your bottom line.

Take your time reading each idea because you will find other ideas nested within them and one idea might spark off another in your mind and don't underestimate the power that small changes can make to your business. As you are reading, be mindful of the Acres of Diamonds story contained within the introduction because you may not realise the full potential of each idea the first time you look. Review this chapter regularly, and keep track of your progress and just like one of your favourite paintings, every time you look at it, you will see something new.

The ideas that follow are not presented in order of importance, this is for you to decide. They are arranged in sections such as things you can do before the customer arrives, things you can do with the job cards and things that you can do in the workshop. Remember that not all of the ideas will be applicable to you now, but circumstances do change and some of them may be more useful to you in the future.

There is a space left at the end of each idea for you to make your own comments and to keep track of your progress. As you read each idea think about why the idea has been suggested and how it can have an impact upon your business. There is also a Quick Reference Check List at the end of this chapter so that you can tick off the ideas as you implement them leaving you with the ideas yet to exploit. Before you begin reading make sure that you are in a comfortable environment so that you can relax and properly digest the information.

THE TIME MACHINE

To make any gains in Utilisation you need to accurately identify non-productive time. This means that your Technicians must have some method for clocking onto a job when they begin and clocking off the job when it is complete. To improve Utilisation, you are interested in the gap that exists between clocking off one job and clocking on to the next job.

At a more advanced level, your Technicians can clock on and off a job for specific reasons such as waiting for parts or obtaining keys for a vehicle from the Sales Department; the amount of detail that you go into is really up to you. However, before you decide to clock on and off everything, please read the following section titled "Eating the Elephant".

Let's get straight to the point. If you do not have a system in place for tracking Idle Time, get one right now, or forget all about any gains that you might be able to achieve with your Utilisation!

There are numerous systems on the market that enable you to track this time ranging from a simple clock card to barcodes and infrared guns. All of them are effective; it's just a matter of which one suits your particular needs.

Date of Implementation:
Comments:

EATING THE ELEPHANT

You will be familiar with the old question of how do you eat an elephant; the answer is of course, a little bit at a time. Keep this thought in your mind because the same is true for improving your Utilisation.

In the previous section entitled The Time Machine, it clearly stated that you need a clock mechanism to identify all of the non-productive time. Unfortunately, in many cases, this is where the problems begin!

The first word of warning here is do not try to achieve everything at once. There's no point in asking your Technicians to clock on and off every single instance of Idle Time such as waiting for parts, locating vehicles, finding special tools etc because that may cause resistance and they may refuse to adopt the process.

Begin simply by clocking on and off each job and then pick one specific sector of Idle Time to monitor each month. For instance, if you believe that your Technicians are spending too much time at the parts counter then you could introduce this aspect to your clocking system. Simply ask your Technicians to clock on and off each job just as they do already and also ask them to clock on and off whilst waiting at the parts counter.

By using this method of performance isolation, you can accurately establish exactly how much time is being spent at the parts counter and therefore how much money it is costing you in lost time. If the problem is significant then you can put the necessary actions in place to reduce this Idle Time and continue to monitor this area.

Here's a helpful word of warning. Don't try to measure five or six different areas of Idle Time at the same time because your Technicians will spend lot's of times clocking on and off each area. This simply leads to your Technicians being frustrated and they will rebel and often refuse to conform. However, in the event that they did clock on and off every area, you would have so much information that it would be difficult to isolate and accurately evaluate.

There are many ideas contained here that I'm sure you will want to implement immediately, but the message here is go easy and isolate one area at a time. How do you eat an Elephant?

Date of Implementation:
Comments:

VEHICLE PARKING
The price of land and business overheads are always on the increase and vehicle parking facilities should not be overlooked. If your customers cannot park, they will become frustrated and you will lose their custom. However, the effect of poor parking facilities is catastrophic on your Utilisation.

When you give a job card to your Technicians, their first task is to locate the vehicle. If the vehicle to be worked on is blocked in behind two other vehicles on the car park, the Technician has to locate the keys for those two vehicles (that's a task in itself) and move them to another location before he can get to the vehicle required. All of this time is lost because you cannot charge the customer. From a motivational standpoint, your Technicians will get frustrated if this is a common occurrence and their frustration will be reflected in the standard of their work and the effects will be shown in productivity, quality control and rectification work; not to mention the devastation on Utilisation.

If you are planning a new development, don't under estimate your parking requirements. The gains you can make with Utilisation will more than cover any investment you may need to make.

If your business is landlocked and you cannot expand, consider renting a portion of a local car park to cope with any overflow that you may have.

Where do your staff park their vehicles? If you are struggling for space, make sure that staff vehicles are parked off-site and make this a condition when recruiting new members of staff. In some instances such as inner cities, it may be viable for you to pay your staff for their parking. Always remember to compare your expense with your gains at Recovery Rate. It's unlikely that staff car parking will cost you £75 per hour, but that is how much you can gain (per Technician) by increasing your Utilisation.

Also to assist with the identification of vehicles in your parking area there are numerous systems on the market ranging from numbered rubber roof cubes to windscreen labels all of which are designed to help the identification of the next vehicle to be worked upon.

Date of Implementation:
Comments:

VEHICLE JOCKEY

Where Idle Time is accurately identified, there are very few Service Departments that have Utilisation higher than 95%. However, the one thing that is common to all of these businesses is the employment of a vehicle jockey.

The vehicle jockey's job is to be a personal assistant to the Technicians and Receptionist. They locate keys and vehicles, load them into the work bays, collect parts, organise consumables, collection and delivery; in short, they conduct all the non-productive duties, which allows the Technicians to continue working productively therefore reducing Idle Time and increasing Utilisation. Your first thoughts are probably focussed on the cost of the additional headcount, but in a Service Department where 6 Technicians are operating, the cost is very easily justified.

Particularly where parking is a problem, a vehicle jockey is a wise investment. All you have to do is ask yourself the question: "During a period of 1 month, how many hours do my Technicians spend locating vehicles before they are able to begin working on them?" When you have the answer, multiply those hours by your Recovery Rate and that will tell you how much more additional revenue you could generate.

Now consider how much a vehicle jockey would cost you for one month. You should now come to the conclusion that this additional revenue should easily cover the cost of a vehicle jockey.

Now comes the part where you really make the gains. Think of all the other non-productive tasks that can be undertaken by this person which will free up your Technicians to continue working productively and you will see the reason why all highly successful Service Departments employ a vehicle jockey. Keep your productives working on productive tasks and you will win.

Date of Implementation:
Comments:

JUST IN TIME SERVICING
This is a practice that is being adopted in dealerships that operate in major cities where parking is a problem, but is also useful for reducing your costs on courtesy vehicles.

If a customer requires a service that takes 1.5 hours to complete, why does the customer need to bring their vehicle in at 8:00 in the morning, take away a courtesy vehicle and return to your dealership at 17:30 in the evening?

The effects of this are that your car park becomes blocked with a vehicle all day and your courtesy vehicle is out all day. This prevents you from booking additional work with people who require a courtesy vehicle.

Is it possible for you to ask your customers to bring their vehicles to you approximately 1 hour before you need them? You can also ask them to collect their vehicles when you have completed the job rather than leaving them parked onsite for the rest of the day.

This idea won't be applicable to all of your customers all of the time, but it will be applicable to some of your customers some of the time. Try it. The alternative is to take the easy route and spend more money on car parking and spend more money on courtesy vehicles; the choice is yours.

Date of Implementation:
Comments:

COLLECTION AND DELIVERY

Whilst conducting a Dealer Principal Master Class in London with a number of franchised dealers, a question arose which followed with an interesting discussion regarding the collection and delivery of customers' vehicles. The conversation was quite entertaining with an interesting outcome so for your enjoyment here is a transcript of the discussion.

J.S. "How do you manage the collection and delivery of your service vehicles?"

S.M. "We use our Technicians because we can't afford the additional cost of another person to do the driving."

J.S. "Do you charge your customers for this service that you provide?"

S.M. "No, of course not."

J.S. "How much does it cost you?"

S.M. "Obviously, the cost is the Technicians salary, but since we are paying them anyway, what difference does it make?"

J.S. "That's an interesting viewpoint; let's explore it a little further. Can you tell me your Recovery Rate please?"

S.M. "Yes, it's £57.36 per hour, why do you ask?"

J.S. "You are right in that the cost of your Technicians time is the amount of money that you pay them, but you have to ask how much money would they have generated if they were working productively during the time they were collecting and delivering. If your Technician had been working productively, he would have been generating at least £57.36 every hour. If he is collecting or delivering he is not generating this money and so this is your true cost of the service that you are providing. Is this correct?"

S.M. "Hmmm, that's a good point, I had not though of it like that before."

J.S. "Also, when your Technician delivers a vehicle to a customer, how do they get back to your dealership?"

S.M. "Another Technician is following behind in another vehicle to bring him back."

J.S. "If you use two Technicians for collection and delivery, the cost to you for providing this service for your customers is your Recovery Rate x 2 which amounts to £114.72 per hour. How many hours per week do your Technicians spend collecting and delivering vehicles?"

S.M. "I'd rather not say! Does anyone here know where I can hire part-time drivers to do my collection and delivery?"

* * * * *

This is a true story and it occurs regularly. Many people fail to realise that the gains in Utilisation are calculated at your Recovery Rate and the potential gains or losses are very significant.

If you do have non-productive people doing your collections and deliveries and you encounter a collection or delivery problem you might consider using a Taxi instead of a Technician because the cost is insignificant compared to the profit that you could be losing.

Only use your Technicians for the purposes that you employed them; don't use them for non-productive tasks such as collection and delivery...unless you charge for it. (Now there's an interesting idea!)

Date of Implementation:
Comments:

PUT YOUR TECHNICIANS WHERE THE WORK IS

What time does your Service Department open for business in the mornings? For the sake of this example, let's say that you open at 8:00 am. The next question is what time do your Technicians turn up for work? Again, let's say 8:00 am. The next question is what time do your customers arrive with their vehicles? Let's say some of them arrive at 8:00 am and others just after that time. Now you can picture the scene.

Here is the crux of the problem. It is not possible to get your workshop fully loaded and productive with all of your Technicians working at 8:00 am, yet you are paying their wages because they are in attendance. All of this time is Idle Time and your Utilisation is being destroyed.

For the sake of easy maths, for this example let's say that you have 8 Technicians. This idea suggests that you consider splitting the start and finish times by half an hour so that you have 4 Technicians arriving at 8:00 am and the other 4 Technicians arriving at 8:30. Obviously, their finish times will also be staggered by half an hour.

This practice of split shifts will help you to avoid the morning chaos, load the workshop effectively and eliminate Idle Time on 4 Technicians who otherwise might be waiting for a job to be allocated. Another benefit is that when the second shift arrives at 8:30, they see the first shift already in action and they get straight to work.

The Receptionist has also had half an hour to get everything ready for the second shift, which means that if a customer is late or does not turn up, you have the time to reschedule the workload without causing Idle Time.

Please read the next idea on internal work loading in conjunction with this idea because it shows the cost of lost opportunity and how both ideas could work very well together

Date of Implementation:
Comments:

INTERNAL LOADING

For the purpose of this example, let's say that your Service Department is open from 08:00 until 17:30. How many of your Technicians are still working productively on your customers' vehicles at 17:00? *The opening hours of your Service Department may differ from this example, but the explanations that follow are still relevant.* You may find that most of the work is completed by 17:00 and the Technicians begin to wash their hands and begin to wind up the

How To Improve Your Utilisation

day's work. This is because customers want their vehicle back the same day and therefore the Technicians cannot begin working on a customer's vehicle and leave the job half finished overnight to complete it the next day.

The solution to this problem is to load all internal work at the latter part of the day because these jobs *can* be left half finished overnight. Your customers are not affected and your Utilisation is improved.

The same rule also applies for first thing in the morning. What happens if your first customer is late? The whole workshop loading process is delayed and Idle Time creeps in again. If you load the first jobs of the day with internal work, you know that they are already on site so your Technicians can begin work immediately. Better still, the internal work could be loaded onto the ramps the evening before.

The potential in this area is colossal and worthy of an example to demonstrate the full impact. For the purpose of this example, let's say that you have 8 Technicians and your Recovery Rate is £75 per hour. Now let's calculate the lost opportunity for this half hour when the Technicians stop working productively

(A) Recovery Rate	= £75
(B) Half hour of labour	= £37.50 (A ÷ 2)
(C) Working days per week	= 6 (inc. Saturday)
(D) Lost opportunity per week	= £225 (B x C)
(E) Working weeks per year	= 44
(F) Lost opportunity per year	= £9,900 (D x E)
(G) Number or Technicians	= 8
(H) **Total Lost Opportunity**	= **£79,200** (F x H)

Your own Recovery Rate may be higher or lower than the figure in this example, so use these formulas with your own Recovery Rate and number of Technicians to calculate your own potentials.

When you have your own figures, realise that this profit goes directly to your bottom line because you are already paying for your Technicians time. Although this is a large figure, keep in mind that it represents only half an hour per day!

It could be that all you have to do to tap into this huge profit potential is to load your workshop beginning with internal work and ending with internal work or implement a split shift system as per the previous idea. You could implement both ideas and gain even more!

Date of Implementation:
Comments:

THE TWILIGHT ZONE
This is an idea specifically for a car dealership as opposed to trucks or motorcycles. It came to me after a discussion with my father who was 77 years old at the time. My wife and I invited him over to eat with us and he refused because by the time he would have finished his meal it would be dark and he said that he does not like driving in the dark.

Naturally, I understand his point and we invited him over for lunch instead. After the conversation had ended, something else occurred to me. I thought about him taking his car to be serviced. Would he take his car to be serviced if it was dark? I asked him the question and he said that he definitely would not take his car to be serviced if he had to drive in the dark.

Now here is an opportunity to be exploited. How many customers do you have on your database that do not like driving in the dark and what special service could you offer them that would mean that they only drive in daylight? How can you tailor that special service to plug up some holes in your Idle Time and therefore increase your Utilisation?

Date of Implementation:
Comments:

IT'S THAT FRIDAY FEELING
Friday is often seen as the end of the working week, often called *"poets day"* and tonight is the night for having a good time. The mentality that usually goes with this mindset is "Let's make sure that we finish on time today."

Check your bookings for Friday afternoons to ensure that they are fully loaded. There is a tendency to under utilise the available time here so that everyone can finish early.

Date of Implementation:
Comments:

LOCKING WHEEL NUTS

Most of the vehicles on the road today have locking wheel nuts to prevent the wheels from being stolen. Unfortunately, they also prevent Technicians from removing them too.

If your customer does not supply the special wheel nut key with the vehicle when it is brought in, the Technician cannot work on the vehicle. All of the time taken to locate the vehicle, load it on to the ramp and then to discover that the wheel nut key is missing is all lost time.

When you take the instructions from your customer, ensure that the locking wheel nut key is with the vehicle, and you know where it is located. It is a simple habit to adopt and could save you a fortune. You could add this idea to your standard booking-in procedure so that it is never overlooked.

Date of Implementation:
Comments:

SELLING UP

When a customer books their vehicle in with you for a straightforward service schedule, what do you do? You could do exactly what the customer has asked you to do, no more, no less, or you could look for additional work that may be required.

The benefit of finding additional work is that you keep the work flowing smoothly and you are able to make more use of your Technicians time. There is a fine balance here though, because it is unwise to find additional work that is not justifiable; finding additional work must be conducted with integrity.

It is wise however, to identify any items that affect the safety of the vehicle, and done properly, your customer will appreciate your diligence and integrity. Proving that you have an effective method for gaining authorisation from your customer to carry out the additional work, this avenue is well worth pursuing.

You can assess whether your Technicians are finding this additional work by tracking the movement of your Parts Sales per Labour Hour. If they are finding additional work on standard servicing schedules, your parts sales per labour hour will show an increasing trend.

Selling up is a matter of habit and good practice for you and your customers. When a vehicle is booked in for a service, your customer might not be aware of any other faults that may exist. You owe it to your customer to thoroughly check the vehicle for them and you owe it to yourself and your business to optimise this opportunity.

Date of Implementation:
Comments:

SERVICE CHECKLIST

OK, you've made up your mind to sell up on service schedules by looking for additional work, but how do you get your Technicians to develop this habit?

One method could be to provide them with a checklist on each service so that the most common items are checked as a matter of routine. Your Technicians can sign the form to confirm that they have checked the specified items and pass it to the Receptionist to gain authorisation for any additional work whilst they continue to work on the vehicle. You can create a simple checklist of your own or download a sample checklist from our web site.

Date of Implementation:
Comments:

CONTACT!

Picture the scene. A customer has left their vehicle with you and taken a courtesy vehicle to continue with the rest of their day. You take the vehicle into the workshop and a Technician finds some additional work that requires authorisation. The customer is not at work today because they have decided to go shopping. You need to contact them to gain their authorisation and most customers have a mobile telephone, but not this one. Now what do you do?

If you have to remove the vehicle from the workshop to carry on with another job and then bring it back in later once you have the necessary authorisation, you will be amassing Idle Time at an alarming rate. This is not a good option and decimates Utilisation.

The solution is to provide your customers with a mobile telephone. OK, get up off the floor! Consider the cost of this lost time and then consider this:

You can purchase mobile telephones on a pay-as-you-go basis, which cost a very small amount, certainly much less than half an hour of your Labour. The telephone companies make their money on these telephones by levying a very high call tariff and this is where you win.

When you give one of these mobile telephones to a customer, set up the telephone so that it can receive in-coming calls, but it cannot make any out-going calls. This means that there will be no further charges for this telephone. Ask your customer to keep the telephone with them so that you can contact them if you need to do so.
You get to contact the customer whenever you need to and you will find that your customers will see this as adding value to their experience with you.

All it will cost you is the initial investment in the telephone and you can use it over and over again to gain authorisations and so improve your Utilisation

Date of Implementation:
Comments:

ASK YOUR TECHNICIANS

There are over 50 ideas in this chapter for improving your Utilisation, but by far the best sources of information that you can tap into are the minds of your own Technicians. Again, this reinforces the point to make the most of, or to utilise the resources that you already have.

Every productive on the shop floor has a wealth of ideas on how you can improve your workflow, but they won't tell you unless you ask them.

Don't assume that they know what you want. Some people don't like to give ideas because they don't want to be seen to be interfering. The idea of passing on information may not even occur to some of your Technicians, and others may not want to come to you because their idea may be wrong and the fear of failure overrides their positive intent.

To overcome these problems you will have to communicate your wishes in the appropriate manner to suit each individual. For some people, a meeting where ideas can be shared and built upon will be ideal, but for others, a quiet chat now-and-again will better suit their level of confidence and contribution.

Other ideas that may work for you are to provide a suggestion box to capture ideas between meetings and also to provide rewards of some kind for the ideas that are successfully implemented.

However, before you go forward with any of these ideas, make sure that everyone fully understands Utilisation by taking the time to explain what you are trying to achieve. When everyone knows what you are trying to achieve the feedback and ideas that you receive will be more valuable.

Date of Implementation:
Comments:

LOCATION OF CONSUMABLES

Every job usually requires consumables of some kind, whether it is a grime pack consisting of paper floor mats, and seat covers or the odd lubrication spray or solvents. The question is where are these consumable items located?

In many cases, the Technician collects the job card and then goes to the Parts counter for the grime pack. He may be served immediately; he may have to wait a few minutes. When the pack is fitted, he proceeds to drive the vehicle into the workshop. After working on the vehicle for a short time he may need a releasing agent to loosen a bolt, so he returns to the parts counter again. He may be served immediately; he may have to wait a few minutes.

A little later he notices a small screw is missing so he returns to the Parts counter. He may be served immediately; he may have to wait a few minutes. And so the story goes on.

All of this waiting around is non-productive time and is costing you a fortune. The money you are losing is not the Technicians salary; it is this time multiplied by your Recovery Rate because you could get another job done in this time if it were not wasted by going in pursuit of consumable items. However, if each Technician has their own supply of consumables on a small trolley unit with wheels, they need not spend any time going backwards and forwards to the Parts Counter because everything would be to hand for them and all the time spent waiting at the Parts Counter for consumables would be eliminated.

But what about security you ask? Each Technician is responsible for their own supply of consumables, which could be topped up each day by a parts operative so that you know exactly how much is being used by each Technician. You can review what is being topped-up whenever you wish. If you have a computer system that aids you in this area, you could then reconcile the consumables charged and used by each Technician.

If you are worried about theft, consider this: The gains you will make are calculated at your Recovery Rate. Therefore if you are able to utilise another 2 hours per week by adopting this practice, and your Recover Rate is £75 per hour, you would gain £150 per week, per Technician. Over 1 year this could add up to additional Labour Sales of at least £6,500 per Technician. How does this figure compare with the value of consumables that may be at risk? And one final question for good measure, how are your consumables being controlled right now?

Date of Implementation:
Comments:

PROVIDE THE KEYS WITH JOB CARD

This is a practice that makes a big difference. When you give the job card to your Technician, make sure that you give him the keys to the vehicle at the same time, especially if it is a vehicle from the Sales Department.

If he doesn't have the keys, he has to go and find them. If it's a Sales vehicle, he'll go and ask the Sales Manager, and he'll send him to a Salesperson and they'll say that they don't know where the keys are! All of this time, the clock is ticking, and your Technicians could be working on other vehicles.

It's a simple process to put in place: When the Sales Department issues you with a job instruction, make it a policy that they also provide you with the keys to the vehicle, and keep those keys locked in your own key cabinet.

If the Sales Department are unable to provide you with the keys at that time, make arrangements to obtain them the day before the job is booked in to the workshop, or refuse to do the job; they'll soon find the keys for you.

Controlling keys from Retail and Fleet customers is a much easier task; just make sure that you give them to your Technicians with the job card.

Date of Implementation:
Comments:

ACCURATE JOB CARD DESCRIPTIONS

How many times have you given the completed invoice to your customer and they say, "You haven't done all of the jobs that I asked you to do".

Where does the problem lie? Well, there are a few things to take into account here, the first of which being that you have missed out on the profit opportunity of additional work. Secondly, you have a disappointed customer on your hands, but the main point for this book is how you can prevent this problem from happening again so that you get your hands on that extra profit that has been offered to you. There are two areas for you to investigate and the second area is covered in the next section. This section deals with the information that is put onto the job card in the first instance.

Are your job card descriptions comprehensive enough for the Technicians to fully understand, or could there be any ambiguity? If there are 3 things that the customer has mentioned, are they numbered on the job card to make them clear?

Example:

1. Carry out 30,000 miles service
2. Water leaking from windscreen seal
3. Check brakes, they are pulling to the left

Once the job is finished and the Technician returns the job card, quickly run through the list with the Technician to ensure that every task has been completed.

It's a simple habit to adopt and at the very least, you owe it to your customers to get it right.

Date of Implementation:
Comments:

CORRECT DIAGNOSIS WITH YOUR CUSTOMER
This section is to be read in conjunction with the previous section. If your customer says that you have not completed all of the jobs that they asked you to do, could it be that the customer thought that they had asked to do the job, but in fact they did not? It could be selective amnesia or a genuine mistake on the part of the customer or the Service Receptionist.

The solution to this problem is to have a simple form that captures all the instructions of the customer. The Receptionist simply writes down all the jobs that are required and the customer signs the form to confirm that they are correct. The information on this form is then transferred to the job card in a clear manner as suggested in the previous idea.

An additional benefit here is when the customer has given you the instructions, ask a simple question such as, "Is there anything else that you would like us to check whilst we are working on your vehicle?" This question prompts the customer to think, and it may jog their memory for something that has been on their mind. You also get additional work!

Finally, when your customer calls to collect their vehicle, the first document that you produce is this form, which they have signed outlining their instructions. You compare this form and your invoice with your customer and when both of them match, the integrity of the customer and the Receptionist is fully protected.

This practice ensures that all work is conducted as the customer originally requested and profit opportunities are not missed out when the Service Reception area is busy.

Date of Implementation:
Comments:

VEHICLE SECURITY SYSTEMS

Most vehicles on the road today have some form of security system fitted and many new vehicles are fitted with keypads that require a password to be entered before you are able to start the engine.

If you give a Technician a job card with the keys for the vehicle and accurate description of customer requirements, but you cannot start the vehicle because you do not have the password for the security system, how much lost time will that cost you?

Make sure that you are in possession of the password when the customer leaves the vehicle with you. As a double check, you could include a section for this (together with locking wheel nuts) on your customer diagnosis forms to serve as a memory jogger.

Date of Implementation:
Comments:

PRE-AGREED AUTHORISATION LIMIT
When your customer leaves their vehicle with you for a service and you find additional work that requires authorisation, what do you do?

Well, of course you attempt to get in touch with your customer by calling the telephone numbers given, but already, Idle Time has sliced another chunk out of your profits and the clock is still ticking.

One solution to this problem is this: When you complete the diagnosis form with your customer, ask a question such as: "If we find any problems that affect the safety of your vehicle, naturally, they will need to be rectified. If it is going to cost a large amount of money, then we will contact you before doing any work, but if it is only a minor item, would you like us to rectify the problem for you so that your vehicle is safe?"

When your customer says "yes" you follow up with: "We'll be happy to do that for you. How much authorisation do you want to give us to complete such a task? Shall we say a maximum of £150?" *It is important to use a figure that is relevant and comfortable for you and the customer.*

When you have your customer's agreement, obtain a signature on your customer diagnosis form and if no additional work is necessary (here's the important bit) *make a point of telling your customer that you have not spent any of the authorised amount!* This will create feelings of trust in the mind of your customer, which is invaluable for repeat business.

If additional work is required, I still recommend that you attempt to contact the customer before you proceed, but if they are unavailable, you have the pre-agreed authorisation limit agreed so you can carry on with the job, workflow is not interrupted and non-productive time is avoided.

Date of Implementation:
Comments:

PRE-RAISE JOB CARDS

Wherever possible, raise the job cards well in advance of the time that they are needed by your Technicians because this will prevent them from hanging around the reception area waiting for the next job.

If it is possible, ask your Receptionist to make this task the last job of the day so that the next morning will flow more smoothly. If they can raise all the job cards for the next morning's work, then the usual morning chaos will be largely diluted and your Technicians will be able to get on with their work rather than queuing up waiting for jobs to be allocated.

Date of Implementation:
Comments:

LOADING EFFICIENCY

Utilisation is governed by workshop loading, but how do you measure your workshop loading? If you have 10 Technicians that clock-in for 8 hours per day, you have 80 Attended Hours that are available to you. The question is how many of those available hours do you book into the workshop each day?

Loading Efficiency is measuring the relationship between the hours booked into the workshop and the Hours Attended.

Example:
(A) Hours booked in w/shop = 88
(B) Hours Attended = 80
(C) Loading Efficiency = **110%** (A ÷ B x 100)

This example shows that there are more hours booked into the workshop than there are hours available to work. This relationship is significant because if your Productivity is greater than 100%, you will have time on your hands that will not be utilised.

Some people only load 90% of capacity "just in case" the additional time is required. This practice is blatantly making the provision for Idle Time and destroys your Utilisation. Beware!

Assess your Loading Efficiency every morning and aim for a loading figure of at least 110%. This will allow for enhanced Productivity because there is a set amount of work to get through and more attention will be given to eliminating your Idle Time and increasing your Utilisation.

From a motivational standpoint, if there is not enough work booked in to the workshop, your Technicians will slow down. However, if they have to work faster to get the days work completed in time, the odds are that they will and every working practice increases.

Date of Implementation:
Comments:

PRE-PICK PARTS

This is a practice from which many dealers receive a large benefit and it's very easy to apply particularly to routine service schedules.

Once you have raised a job card, you will generally know what parts have to be fitted with each job, therefore if you liaise with the Parts Departments they can gather the parts required and put them into a cardboard box ready to give to the Technician when he collects the job card. The parts are also booked onto the job for invoicing ready for when the work is complete. This practice means that your Technicians do not spend any time waiting for parts and your Receptionist is not delayed by waiting for parts information to be put on the invoice. This entire process means that Idle Time is kept to a minimum.

Date of Implementation:
Comments:

LOCATION OF SPECIAL TOOLS

Most Service Departments have a tool board mounted on the wall to house the special tools. Behind the tool, there is usually a silhouette of the tool painted onto the tool board so that you can see where each of the tools is kept. The question here is when you look at your special tools board, how many tools can you see and how many silhouettes can you see?

If you have purchased special tools but your Technicians cannot find them when they need them, the time spent searching for them is all dead time.

There are a few simple solutions to this one, first of all take a photograph of the tool board when it is full, enlarge the photograph and mount it next to the board so that everyone can see where each of the tools is located. It may be an idea to laminate the photograph so that it does not get damaged by oily fingerprints.

You can also charge your workshop Foreman with the responsibility of ensuring that your Technicians return the tools to their rightful place when they have finished with them.

Also ensure that the tool board is fully stocked at close of business ready for when the business opens the next day. It's another simple habit to adopt that could save you a fortune in time as well as special tools.

Date of Implementation:
Comments:

AVAILABILITY OF SPECIAL TOOLS
Do you have particular special tools that are in frequent use? If so, do you have enough of those special tools on hand or do your Technicians have to wait for them to become available?

The best solution is to ask your Technicians about this one, they should be able to tell you if you need more than the current supply of a particular special tool.

However, before you invest any money, make sure that you have implemented the previous idea because it would be pointless spending money on tools that are unavailable simply because they have not been returned to their rightful place.

Date of Implementation:
Comments:

WORKING BY REMOTE CONTROL

When a Technician is given the next vehicle to repair, he drives the vehicle to the workshop, but who opens the workshop door for him? Sometimes they toot the horn and another Technician downs tools and opens the door. The downside here is that the Technician who opened the door has had his work disrupted and may have lost his train of thought.

A simple solution is to have the workshop door opened and closed by remote control. A sensor fitted to the door mechanism together with a remote control for <u>each</u> Technician would cost very little money and solve this problem instantly.

If you think about how many times the workshop door is opened and closed each day (don't forget road tests) you can imagine how many times work flow is disrupted by some else wanting access in or out of the workshop.

You could also think about the money you would save on heating bills too because the door will be closed much quicker after it has been opened.

Date of Implementation:
Comments:

THE TOOL MAN

I'll not mention brand names, but you know who they are! They pull up on site in a large van kitted out with toolboxes and tools for your Technicians to buy.

When the tool man arrives, the workshop empties in an instant for 1 of 2 possible reasons:

1. Your Technicians want to buy some tools
2. They are hiding because they owe him money

To get a result with Utilisation, you must prevent such interruptions at all cost! If your workshop stops dead in its tracks, whatever has caused this is costing you a fortune. The arrival of the tool man is one of the causes of these problems. A solution to this could be to get the tool man to arrive at an appointed time to suit you; after all, it is your business!

When the van arrives, arrange for the Technicians to visit him in an orderly fashion, let's say in pairs for instance. Under no circumstances should you allow them all to go out of the workshop together because the workshop will stop dead in its tracks. It is a problem that must be controlled and managed effectively. Alternatively, you could always arrange to have the tool man arrive at lunchtime or the end of the day when the workflow cannot be interrupted.

This same philosophy applies to the sandwich van. Let one person take the sandwich orders, probably an apprentice because this prevents letting everyone out to stand in an orderly line waiting to be served and leaving your workshop dead in its tracks.

Date of Implementation:
Comments:

WAITING AT THE PARTS COUNTER

One large segment of wasting time is for your Technicians to be waiting for parts at the back counter. As previously suggested, you could pre-pick the parts for each job to prevent waiting, but this is not practical on every job; what happens on jobs where the parts have not been pre-picked? The first question to be answered is do you have sufficient parts personnel to cope with the workshop demand? If the answer is yes, then you might want to consider how do your parts personnel know when there is a Technician waiting for parts?

A simple solution could be to have a bell installed at the counter to notify the Parts personnel that they are required. Obviously, discretion is required on the part of your Technicians here, especially if the bell can be heard in the customer facing areas.

If the bell continues to ring without being answered, then you may wish to reconsider whether you have sufficient parts personnel.

Alternatively, another solution could be that if the parts personnel are busy, then the Technician could leave the job card at the counter on a clipboard and continue with the job. When parts personnel are free, they can read the job card and take the required parts to the Technician. This idea will not apply in every set of circumstances, but it will apply to some of them.

Date of Implementation:
Comments:

WORKSHOP LAYOUT

The positioning of your work bays is critical to the flow of the work going through the workshop. In many cases, vehicles go in and out of the same door and this two-way traffic often causes disruption and congestion as some vehicles have to be moved in the busier times of the day. All of this additional vehicle movement is Idle Time and is eating into your profits.

Where it is possible, the best solution here is to have a one-way traffic system in operation so that vehicles come in through one door and go out through another door at the opposite end of the workshop. This prevents vehicles travelling in opposite directions in the same area of the workshop.

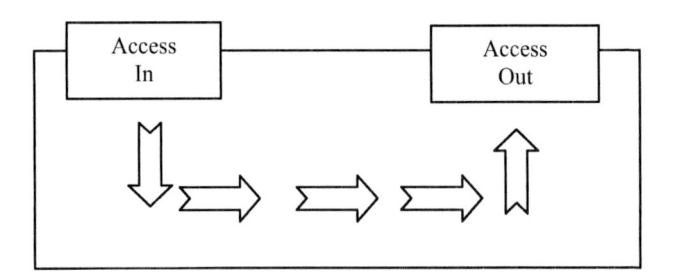

If a one-way system is not possible for your current circumstances, you could still consider the layout of the workshop as a whole.

- Do vehicles have to be moved at anytime for other vehicles to gain access?

- Are the special tools and diagnostic equipment in easily accessible areas?

- What is the level of teamwork; do your Technicians genuinely help each other?

- Does the layout of your workshop help or hinder the flow of work?

Any one of these activities will make an improvement to your performance, but if you implement all of them you will have a significant improvement.

Date of Implementation:
Comments:

WALKING THE PIT LANE
In 1988 I attend my first Formula 1 Grand Prix and I was fortunate enough to have a pass that allowed me to access the Pits. As I walked along the Pit Lane admiring the cars, the drivers and the hive of activity going on around them, there was one thing that really struck me as outstanding. The thing that I found amazing was the condition of the floor and working area in every one of the Pit Garages; I was truly stunned at how clean they were!

As I stood there looking on, a car sprouted a fluid leak. The car was fixed and the working area was cleaned up immediately in readiness for the next job.

If the working areas were not as pristine as they were, the Technicians would be tripping over discarded items and getting frustrated because they would have to keep moving obstacles out of their way. One of the aims of a Formula 1 team is to eliminate as many obstacles as possible and for the Technicians, a clean and tidy workshop is an essential part of the strategy to get their car into the race.

You are in a race for profit then make no mistake about it; a clean and tidy workshop is just as essential part of your strategy as it is for the Formula 1 teams.

Walk around your workshop and take an objective look at the cleanliness of the working areas. How will the current conditions affect your Technicians? Do they have sufficient light? What is the "mood" of the workshop? Take care to notice obstacles that might get in their way such as airlines trailing across the floor instead of being properly mounted on the wall, discarded trolley jacks, discarded parts packaging, overflowing rubbish bins, location of waste oil drums, locations of oil and water lines, etc.

Your aim is to remove any obstacles that might exist so that work can flow through without encountering any unnecessary problems. Consider making this "Pit Lane walk" a part of your everyday routine so that cleanliness and tidiness becomes part of your workshop culture.

Date of Implementation:
Comments:

ACCESS TO TECHNICAL DATA

Where do you keep your reference manuals and computers for the access of technical data? The more time your Technicians spend searching for information or technical data the more time is being wasted and of course your Utilisation diminishes.

An easy method of reducing this downtime is to erect proper shelving to house your technical manuals and to keep them maintained as you would a library. Make sure that your Technicians can gain access to them easily and they are maintained in an orderly fashion for future reference.

You can imagine what it would be like if you went to your local library to find some specific information and you found a pile of books in the corner of a room. How much time would you spend looking through all of the books before you found the one that you need? Think of all that wasted time and also think about your mood and state of mind and how that would affect your work.

It may take a little time to erect the shelving and properly categorise your manuals, but think about how often you will use them and how much time will be saved in the future. When you decide to adopt this idea, also adopt the idea of having a system for your Technicians to put them back in the right place when they have finished with them!

Date of Implementation:
Comments:

ACCESS OF TECHNICIANS TO CUSTOMERS

Numerous surveys conducted by manufacturers have come up with the suggestion that customers would like to speak with the Technician that has been working on their vehicle. You must decide for yourself whether this is a good practice for you to adopt or not. If you believe that your customers want to speak with your Technicians, do you think that your customers will be happy to pay for that time?

The answer is probably no, which means that you have a dilemma on your hands because you will be creating Idle Time and reducing Utilisation. There are four options for this scenario:

1. Agree with the survey results and allow your Technicians to meet with your customers and don't charge them for the privilege. The problem here is that you increase Idle Time or reduce Productivity depending on how you account for this time. The downside is that you have no control over this area because it is not itemised.

2. Disagree with the survey results and do not make your any changes to the way that you run your business. The question here is who is currently speaking with your customers and are your customers happy with this arrangement?

3. Agree with the survey results and add an additional line to your Direct Expenses that will capture the time spent with customers so that you

can separate this time from Idle Time. This will provide you with the true cost of your Technicians meeting with your customers so that you can assess the value of this practice.

4. Be open-minded about the survey results and test its integrity by charging your customer for this "productive" time. This will increase your Labour Sales and profitability and give you the truth about whether your customers really value meeting with your Technicians.

Everyone has an opinion, but because all businesses are different, there is no definitive answer. Perhaps these surveys should ask the Technicians if they want to be made available to customers because not all Technicians are willing to meet with customers. You will need to carefully consider each option before you proceed with any of them.

Date of Implementation:
Comments:

TEA BREAKS
Do your Technicians clock off their jobs when they are on a tea break? If they do not, then your Utilisation will be overstated because they will be shown to be working productively during this time and your true Utilisation will be hidden from view.

In an experiment I conducted with a dealership, the Technicians were told that structured tea breaks were no longer in place and they can now take a break whenever they wish. Brave move you might say, but here are the results:

All of the Technicians used to take a tea break at the same time, which meant that the flow of work stopped dead in its tracks for at least 20 minutes. When the new rules came into effect, the Technicians usually took their break at the end of a job rather than part way through. The chances of all of the Technicians completing their jobs all at the same time is very unlikely, which meant that the tea breaks no longer stopped the work flow dead in its tracks and Idle Time was significantly reduced.

If you have a set tea break at 10:00am what time do your Technicians begin to get ready for their tea break? If the tea break is scheduled to finish at 10:10am, what time do they return to the workshop? In many cases, the answer is at least 5 minutes each side of the tea break and if you have 8 Technicians, two tea breaks and lunchtime, then the amount of non-productive time is at least 20 hours per week. If your Recovery rate is £70 then the annual cost is somewhere in the order of £64,400 per year.

Now don't think about banning tea breaks altogether because there are laws against such actions and you certainly do not want to treat your Technicians like robots do you?

The solution is to control this time by staggering tea breaks across the workforce in such a way that the workshop does not stop dead in its tracks.

Date of Implementation:
Comments:

DIAGNOSING THE PROBLEM
How much time do your Technicians spend diagnosing faults for your customers? Do you charge your customers for this time?

Most manufacturers will not allow you to charge them for diagnosis on warranty work, but don't let those policies set the precedent for any diagnosis that is not warranty work. If you think that a charge is fair and reasonable, then charge for diagnosis. If you don't ask, you don't get!

Date of Implementation:
Comments:

IDENTIFYING THE PROBLEM
If you do not have a comprehensive computer system for identifying your Idle Time, you may encounter a few problems with your Technicians clocking on and off jobs when waiting for parts and other such tasks. However, rather than tackle every problem area at the

same time, deal with them individually. This method produces benefits in two areas.

1. It is easy to clock on and off one area
2. Everyone focuses on solving the problem in that specific area

Here's how you can get started. Let's be controversial with this example and say that you have a specific problem with internal work.

The Sales team give you a repair order, but they are not supplying you with the keys to the vehicle. When you issue the job card to the Technician, he cannot find the keys and the Sales person concerned is with a customer. Now your lost time is escalating because your Technician is not productive and it is really the fault of the Sales Department, but what can you do about it?

Here's how to identify an isolated area such as this. When you issue the job to the Technician, clock on with <u>two</u> job cards. Only when the Technician is in possession of the keys and the vehicle, clock off the <u>first</u> card. When the job is complete, clock off the second card. Here's why you want to do this:

The first card will show you how much time has been spent locating keys and the vehicle; this could easily be 15 minutes. All of this time you could have been working on another vehicle and earning revenue!

Now let's be really controversial. Because this lost time is the fault of the Sales Department, charge them for it! A number of things will happen.

1. The Sales Manager will kick and scream about the additional cost. However, now you have his attention, explain why it is so important for you to have the keys and the vehicle in the first place.

2. You will realise yourself the real cost of wasted time.

3. You will solve the problem of obtaining keys and vehicles from the Sales Department.

You can use this "additional card" method for identifying many other areas of your Idle Time. You don't have to attack everything all at once, take your time and address each problem systematically.

Date of Implementation:
Comments:

CLEANING UP AFTER A JOB
After each job is finished, who cleans up the mess around the ramp or the pit afterwards? If this is a job that your Technicians undertake, then you have two choices here:

1. Do nothing and ignore the profit opportunity
2. Charge the customer for the time

If you do nothing, this time is non-productive and prevents more work coming through. However, you might have laughed when you read option 2 and said something like, "Oh yes, you try charging the customer for cleaning up".

Let's work on option 2 here because that's where the additional profits are. This is a problem that is particularly prevalent within the truck industry and the main problem is fear. Most Receptionists are too afraid to add this to the bill because of what the customer *might* say. There is a simple rule in life that says, "if you don't ask, you don't get" and that fits this scenario perfectly.
Whilst conducting a consultancy visit at a dealership I noticed how much time the Technicians were spending cleaning up after certain jobs so I put this suggestion forward.

The Receptionist was outraged and said, "We can't do that, our customers will tell me what to do with the bill!" After a little cajoling, the Receptionist was still reluctant, but nevertheless, he agreed to try it.

The result was that some customers understood the situation and paid the bill, whilst some customers refused to pay and the amount was deducted from the invoice.

The point is that this idea did not work for all of the customers all of the time, but it did work for some of the customers some of the time and in this case more than £10,000 was added straight to the bottom line over the period of 1 year.

If it is the customers mess that has to be cleaned up then is it fair and reasonable to charge that customer for the time taken to clean up that mess? Is this a question of ethics, or is it a question of fear? Only you can decide.

Date of Implementation:
Comments:

INTERDEPARTMENTAL RELATIONSHIPS
OK, let's understand what I mean here…I'm not talking about your Sales Manager courting your Service Receptionist because those kind of relationships are covered in other kinds of books! My point here is that the working relationships between departments has a huge impact upon your operational performance. Does your management team work together towards one company objective, or does each manager fight for their department at the cost of the others?

When your management team work together and understand each other's role, then improving operational performance becomes much easier to achieve. If they do not work together then more problems are created than are solved.

To improve interdepartmental relationships, ensure that each of your managers has an understanding of how the other departments function. This knowledge is critical for management meetings because if the Sales manager does not understand how the Service

Department functions, then they will not understand how they can help.

I have been in many management meetings where the Sales Manager "switches off" when the Service Manager is talking simply because the terminology used sounds like a foreign language and they don't understand. It's not their fault; they just haven't been trained in the subject.

This is not limited to Sales Managers! How many people do you work with that could be more helpful to you, but maybe they just don't understand? When they do understand, relationships improve and so too does your operational performance. Arrange a special meeting with these people and teach them about your business. If they know the *reason* for doing something, you will get much more co-operation.

Date of Implementation:
Comments:

PARTS V.O.R. CONTENT
You already know that when something happens in one department has a direct effect upon the other departments in your business. Service and Parts departments have to work closely together and the profile of the parts stock is paramount for the right supply of parts to your workshop.

If the parts profile is wrong, then the chances are that the parts required in the workshop will not be in stock and this means that the parts will have to be ordered on an emergency basis so that they arrive next day.

This emergency ordering of parts is referred to as V.O.R. (Vehicle Off Road). The higher the VOR%, the worse your Utilisation will be because this means that you could be partway through a repair and then work stops while waiting for parts. What do you do with the vehicle? Do you leave it in a bay and lose the productive space or do you put the vehicle back together so that you can move it? Either way you lose productive time, which means that you would be well advised to keep a regular check on the VOR%.

You will need to liaise with your Parts Manager on a regular basis to ensure that you have the right parts profile to meet your needs because VOR% is dependent upon the frequency of your parts stock order. It is also a good idea to review the parts ordering parameters on your parts computer system because it is often this system that dictates your stock profile.

Keep a register of the type of parts that cause problems in the workshop because of VOR and then periodically, use your register as a point of discussion with your Parts Manager to assist with parts profiling.

Date of Implementation:
Comments:

SET A TARGET AND GIVE REGULAR FEEDBACK

When your team knows what Utilisation is all about, set a target for it. Tell them exactly what you want to achieve and give them the tools to achieve it.

Now here's the important part. Once you have given the target make sure that you provide regular feedback on their progress. This could be a graph on the wall showing the increasing trend, a short weekly letter, a copy of your daily operating controls or a short meeting every few weeks.

If you don't give any feedback the whole idea will fizzle out and be branded as the latest fad. On the other hand, giving feedback keeps their interest alive and maintains their focus on thinking about solutions.

Feedback is the breakfast of champions, when you make the effort to inform others, they will make the effort to inform you. If you fail to inform others, they will fail to inform you.

Date of Implementation:
Comments:

MEASURING THE CURRENT AVERAGE

So far, we have only discussed measuring Utilisation as an overall departmental statistic, whereas you could measure the Utilisation of each of your Technicians. However, beware of the performance blind that get drawn over your eyes!

If someone performs well at any endeavour we have a tendency to think of them as always being good at that skill. Even when their performance begins to subside, we always seem to remember the good times and we fail to see the performance decline.

One measuring method you can use to avoid this "good time" blind is to measure the current average. Instead of producing snapshot figures each month, consider producing a figure on a rolling 90-day basis so that the figure that is produced gives you the average performance over the last 90-day period. If someone has a bad month, they will have to produce much higher results in the months that follow to ensure that their average performance is restored.

By measuring the current average of each of your Technicians you will keep their mind on the task in hand because one bad month will be evident in their average for the whole of the 90-day period.

Date of Implementation:
Comments:

MARKETING
You can only improve Utilisation if you have enough work to fill your Idle Time. The way in which you acquire more work is down to how you market your Service Department.

Marketing is not just advertising in the local press or producing a glossy brochure, it's a whole host of activities that work together to build your business. In fact it's the subject of another book in this series; watch this space! Before you get your hands on that book, here are some "marketing musts" for you to consider right now:

- Whether you realise it or not, most of your business comes from referral, but do you have a structured referral system in place?

- Do you have an effective Service Reminder system?

- Do you have a structured telesales operation for customer follow up?

- Are you managing your database effectively?

- Do you have a customer loyalty programme?

- Do you sell Service Plans and budget schemes?

There are indeed many things to be considered here because marketing is such a large subject. However, here are some questions for you to answer that might stimulate further ideas:

- When your customers think about their vehicle, do they think about you?

- What can you do to strengthen your links with your customers?

- What can you do to prevent customer attrition?

Take your time answering these questions, and also pose these questions to your team. Remember that you don't own your customers; you only borrow them from your competition.

Date of Implementation:
Comments:

TRAINING
Now I'm not trying to do myself out of any work here, but it's important for you to realise that it's not always up to someone else to do your training for you; you can do it yourself.

If you want to make gains in Utilisation, you have to educate everyone and tell them "what" you are trying to achieve and "why" you are trying to achieve it.

If you don't tell anyone what you want them to do and why you want them to do it, they will not see the benefits. You will encounter resistance and it will be very difficult for you to make a difference.

One solution is to hold a meeting to explain what you want to achieve with Utilisation. If you need some help explaining the benefits of Utilisation, there is an audio programme that accompanies this book, which you can use to stimulate your meeting; all you need is a CD player. The programme is available from our web site.

Here's an important point to keep in mind. Do not use the meeting for any other reason; keep the content solely on the subject of Utilisation for maximum impact.

After your meeting has concluded, write up a summary of the meeting together with any agreed action plans and give a copy to everyone who has attended your meeting. Don't confuse this idea with producing meeting minutes; you must be clear in your objectives and give clear instructions in the form of agreed action plans.

If your team do not know what you want, how will they achieve it? If your team does not understand Utilisation (and the chances are that they don't), then it's up to you to train them.

Take the initiative on this one because the additional benefit is that you too will also learn a great deal more about Utilisation in the process.

Date of Implementation:
Comments:

DEBTOR DAYS
Did you know that 80% of businesses are foreclosed within their first 5 years of trading? It is an alarming result and it's because many businesses simply run out of cash because all of their money is tied up in their customers' hands. This money is shown on your accounts as Debtors.

The average amount of time it takes your customers to pay you is called Debtors days. Ideally, you want your Debtor Days to be less than 45 days and if it is higher, this means that you are waiting longer to receive your money from your customers, which means that you have to invest more of your own money in your business.

If you do not have this additional cash to invest in your business, it could mean that you encounter cash-flow problems and your suppliers may be difficult with you. This in turn could have a negative effect on your Utilisation because you may not be able to obtain parts or other materials at the time when you need them.

Credit control is critical in all businesses because the availability of cash is the thing that allows you to continue trading. If you are part way through repairing a vehicle and you need a part from a supplier that has your account on stop, the progress on the vehicle is halted, which decreases utilisation and non-productive time gains a stronger hold. Here are some things to consider:

- Are your Debtor days around 45 days or less?
- Do you check your W.I.P. at least once a week?
- Are your cash accounts actually paid in cash?
- Do you have good relationships with suppliers?

One business that I work with has a rule that states that if any cash sales are not fully paid within 5 days, then no bonus will be paid to the Service Manager.

You will not be surprised to learn that in their case, no cash sales find their way on to the Debtors list.

Date of Implementation:
Comments:

Up Close And Personal
The chances are that you have a business card, but the question here is do your Technicians have a business card?

Imagine that you have just had some work done on your vehicle and you have pay your bill and you are ready to drive away. When you get inside your vehicle you notice a professionally printed hanger suspended from your rear view mirror saying something such as the following:

My name is David Jones and I am the Technician that has worked on your vehicle today.

If you are happy with the work that I have done for you, and you would prefer me to work on your vehicle next time, please inform the Service Receptionist when you book in your vehicle with us.

Thank you very much for your custom.

At first, you might think that this practice could be very restrictive, but in fact, the opposite is true because this idea accomplishes a number of tasks .
Firstly, your Technician is putting his name in front of the customer and he is saying that "I did this to your vehicle". What do you think will happen to quality control and the cleanliness of the vehicle?

Secondly, you can have the mirror hanger printed with all of your company details, telephone numbers and web site addresses and there is a very good chance that your customer will keep the card because he wants the same Technician to work on his vehicle next time. Also, with computer technology and ink jet printer quality being so good, you can even personalise the card with your customers name to make him feel really special because it is customer care such as this that earns referrals for you..

Thirdly, when your customer returns to have more work carried out and he informs you of the Technician he would like to work on his vehicle, you now have the option to load your workshop more effectively. For instance, if he wants his vehicle booked in for Wednesday to be worked on by David Jones, you have the option to accept his request or you can say that David is fully booked on Wednesday, but you can fit him in on Thursday or whatever day suits your workshop loading for that particular job.

The end result is that you have the opportunity to load the workshop more effectively, your customer feels more comfortable and confident when booking his vehicle in, and the point is that you will get more work because your customers will come back and they will speak to others about this service.

Don't be surprised when you have new customers come to you asking for their vehicle to worked on by a specific Technician who has been recommended by a friend! Give this some thought. When you are given a recommendation has anyone ever said to you "and make sure that you ask for so and so"?

Referrals with a persons name are far more powerful than a recommendation to a business. The cost of printing and the small amount of effort that you need to put into this initiative will produce lots more work for you in the future.

Date of Implementation:
Comments:

DO YOU HAVE ENOUGH SUPPORT?
Are any of your Technicians getting involved in non productive administration tasks or do they have enough support to take care of these things so that they can continue with productive work? The way to establish this is to measure your Productive ratio. This ratio simply compares the number of productive people with the number of non-productive people.

Typically, non-productive people could be the Service Manager, Service Receptionist and Warranty

Clerk and of course the productive people are your Technicians. To establish your Productive Ratio you simply divide the number of productives by the number of non-productives and express the result as a ratio.

Example:
(A) Productive staff   = 12
(B) Non-Productive staff   = 4
(C) **Productive : Non Productive = 3:1**   (A ÷ B)

Most manufacturers' Composite results appear to average at around 3:1, or in other words, for every 3 Technicians that you employ, you have 1 member of staff who is non-productive. If your ratio was reading at 6:1 this might suggest that you do not have sufficient non-productive support for your Technicians and they will be involved in non-productive tasks which of course reduces your Utilisation.

This statistic can vary wildly and is dependent upon how you apportion your Apprentices and Foreman. Obviously, if your Productive Ratio is lower than 3:1 this might suggest that you have too many non productive staff for the size of the business that you are operating. You have to decide whether your Technicians have enough support to prevent them getting tied up with non-productive administration tasks.

Date of Implementation:
Comments:

CAN YOU DO IT?

The industry is changing and what we did in the past may not be relevant today. Workshops are not as busy as they were 10 years ago and so we need to exploit every opportunity that comes in. With this thought in mind, have you taken a second look at the amount of sub contract work that you are giving away?

Over the past few years the re-gassing of air conditioning units was seen to be a specialist job, but now with a small investment in the equipment you can take on this task yourself and with almost every vehicle having air conditioning fitted it may be a worthy investment for you to consider for the future. How many other jobs do you sub contract out to other companies that you could do yourself? Take a fresh look at all of the sub contract invoices that you have generated over the past six months and see if you can establish a common area that you could exploit. If you can feed more jobs into your working day the better your Utilisation will be.

Date of Implementation:
Comments:

THE GHANDI PRINCIPLE

Ghandi said "You cannot understand another man until you have walked a mile in his moccasins". He was of course a man of great influence who spent much of his time thinking of things from the other persons' perspective. You could take this to mean that you cannot understand a problem unless you have experienced it yourself. If you think of a solution to a problem without understanding the practicalities surrounding it, then you could be wasting your time.

One of the best ways to discover what is happening at a practical level in your workshop is to see it through the eyes of the job card. To do this you must become the job card, in other words you must follow the path of the job card through every step so that you can fully understand what happens at every junction.

Start this process right from the beginning where a customer is booked into the system and a job card is produced. Keep the job card in your hand the whole time and walk through every step from allocation to the Technician, clocking onto the job, clocking on and off sectors of Idle Time, clocking off the job, Technicians write up and of course right through the invoicing procedures to its final conclusion. Don't underestimate the power of this exercise because you will find out much more about your business than you think and you will then understand how to implement your new ideas to best effect without shaking the foundations of the systems that already exist. When you walk a mile in the moccasins of the jobs card, you will have a much greater understanding of what is needed.

Date of Implementation:
Comments:

IMPROVING YOUR UTILISATION
CROSS-REFERENCE CHECK LIST

The Time Machine ☐
Eating The Elephant ☐
Vehicle Parking ☐
Vehicle Jockey ☐
Just In Time Servicing ☐
Collection And Delivery ☐
Put Your Technicians Where The Work Is ☐
Internal Loading ☐
The Twilight Zone ☐
It's That Friday Feeling ☐
Locking Wheel Nuts ☐
Selling Up ☐
Service Checklist ☐
Contact! ☐
Ask Your Technicians ☐
Location Of Consumables ☐
Provide The Keys With Job Card ☐
Accurate Job Card Descriptions ☐
Correct Diagnosis With Your Customer ☐
Vehicle Security Systems ☐
Pre-Agreed Authorisation Limit ☐
Pre-raise job cards ☐
Loading Efficiency ☐
Pre-Pick Parts ☐
Location Of Special Tools ☐
Availability Of Special Tools ☐
Working By Remote Control ☐
The Tool Man ☐
Waiting At The Parts Counter ☐
Workshop Layout ☐

Walking The Pit Lane ☐
Access To Technical Data ☐
Access Of Technicians To Customers ☐
Tea Breaks ☐
Diagnosing The Problem ☐
Identifying The Problem ☐
Cleaning Up After A Job ☐
Interdepartmental Relationships ☐
Parts V.O.R. Content ☐
Set A Target And Give Regular Feedback ☐
Measuring The Current Average ☐
Marketing ☐
Training ☐
Debtor Days ☐
Up Close and Personal ☐
Do You Have Enough Support? ☐
Can You Do It? ☐
The Ghandi Principle ☐

Carefully cross reference this check list with your progress to ensure that you maximise all of these ideas on how you can improve your Utilisation. Don't make the mistake of ticking them off before you read them and thinking that you understand what the title might suggest. Only tick off an idea when you have implemented it into your business and the ideas that are left open will show how much more potential there is in your reserves. Be aware that some of these ideas will be applicable to your business today, and others might be more applicable to your business as it develops and grows. Keep in mind that this list is not meant as a memory jogger because there are other ideas nested within many of these that are not listed. You will need to read each idea independently to fully understand the power of its application.

To conclude this chapter I'll leave you with a final thought. Improving Utilisation can be one of the most difficult things to achieve in your business because it demands a great deal of determination and patience. The results are aimed at a long-term objective, not an overnight success. The good news is that once you achieve your long-term objectives, you will continue to reap your rewards month after month after month, all you need is a little patience in the short-term. You will need to implement your actions and patiently sit back and wait.

With time and patience
the mulberry leaf becomes a silk gown

- Chinese Proverb

CHAPTER VI

HOW TO IMPROVE YOUR PRODUCTIVITY

*"The people who get on in this world
are the people who get up and look
for the circumstances they want and
if they can't find them, they make them."*

- George Bernard Shaw

VI

HOW TO IMPROVE YOUR PRODUCTIVITY

Productivity is all about the relationship between Hours Sold and Hours Worked and to improve your Productivity you must either increase your Hours Sold or decrease your Hours Worked.

In almost all cases your Productivity is improved by decreasing the number Hours Worked by beating the allocated time given for the job whilst the Hours Sold remains the same. There are only a few occasions where you are able to increase the Hours Sold because the cost of most jobs are agreed with your customers before you are given the work by means of menu pricing and customer quotations. In the main, the ideas that follow are focussing on the reduction of Hours Worked so that your Technicians are able to beat the allocated job times. Whilst you may already have some of these ideas in place you will find other new ideas that will compliment your workshop. keep in mind that small changes make a big difference.

You may also notice that there are some ideas listed in this chapter that are very similar to some of the ideas shown for improving your Utilisation, but they will be in this section for slightly different reasons. You will find real profit gains when you can identify these common ideas because you will be elevating both Utilisation and Productivity at the same time.

BAD WORKMEN AND THEIR TOOLS

You will have heard the saying that a bad workman always blames his tools, but if you are measuring your Productivity then the right tool for the job will make a significant difference.

Every manufacturer produces special tools for their vehicles but the question here is do you have all the special tools that you need at your disposal?

Before you respond with an automatic 'yes of course we have all the special tools', go and check. Ask your Technicians if you are in need of any special tools, and also check to see that the special tools that you do have are in good working order. It's well worth conducting this special tool check at least once every month. If you take on a job that requires the use of a special tool which you do not have or the special tool is broken, your Productivity will suffer and the profit that you lose here could be significantly more than the cost of keeping your special tools well stocked and maintained. It also sends a positive message to your technicians too.

Date of Implementation:
Comments:

TOOL DIVERSITY

OK, so you have all the manufacturer's special tools in place, but do you have enough of them?

There are occasions where you could have three Technicians requiring a special tool at the same time. When you conduct your audit to ensure that you have the necessary special tools, you also need to consider the diversity of them. The best way to find out this information is to ask your Technicians if they are ever left waiting for a special tool that someone else is using. If this happens frequently, it is well worth investing in additional special tools of this kind so that you prevent the time that is being wasted whilst waiting.

Date of Implementation:
Comments:

THE RIGHT MAN FOR THE JOB

Productivity is all about completing the job in a faster time than is charged, therefore if you have one Technician who is particularly good in a specific area, let's say fitting clutches, then it makes sense to give that Technician all of work on clutches because he will complete those jobs more quickly than anyone else and therefore increase your Productivity by reducing the Hours Worked.

Of course it's not only clutches that you focus on, you will have Technicians who are good at one type of work and not so good on others. Your skill is to make sure that you put the right Technician with the most appropriate skills onto the right job. If you just allocate any job to any Technician you run the risk of some Technicians not knowing the task as well as others and they might take more time to complete the job and your Productivity will reduce and therefore it stands to reason that putting the right man on the right job will increase your Productivity.

The question now is does your Receptionist or whoever hands out the jobs in your workshop know the skills and knowledge base of each Technician? You might want to conduct a skills analysis on each of your Technicians to ensure that you are doing them all justice and to make certain that you have the right information so that you can accurately identify the right man for the right job.

Date of Implementation:
Comments:

TECHNICAL TRAINING
Following on from the previous section, once you have conducted the skills analysis on your team you will be aware of the strengths and weaknesses within your workshop. However, there is a downside to loading your workshop by giving the jobs to those who have the appropriate skills because you will create specialists in certain areas of technical expertise and you will not spread those skills around your workshop. This means that could you become dependant upon a certain Technician to complete certain tasks which might limit your ability to take on more of this kind of work and you could be at risk of losing that kind of work if a Technician leaves your company.

The objective here is to achieve balance. Yes, you do need to give the right job to the right man, but you also have to consider how you are going to spread those skills around the workshop. Don't get caught up in the delusion of achieving short-term gains in Productivity, think about the technical training that is required and how you are going to conduct that training. Sometimes you have to lose a battle in order to win the war. Technical training is essential for improving your Productivity and also the long-term future of your Technicians, but make sure that you are getting the right technical training for the right man; consider the balance of your workshop as a whole.

Date of Implementation:
Comments:

COMMERCIAL TRAINING

Ok, we've discussed the Technical training for your Technicians, but what about commercial training for you and your management team? The only way to improve your Productivity is if you AND your management team fully understand what Productivity really is. One of the biggest problems you may encounter is conveying all of these ideas to others within your team. If they do not fully understand what Productivity is and how it is calculated they will not understand your ideas and as a result you may encounter resistance to change.

You can enrol your staff onto professional training programmes, or if you are already fully conversant with Productivity, you can provide the training yourself. Whichever route you decide is best for you, it is critical that everyone knows what you are trying to achieve, why you are trying to achieve it and what you expect along the way. If your team is not fully aware of the commercial aspects of Productivity your efforts will fall at the first hurdle. People need to know where they are going <u>before</u> they embark upon the journey.

Date of Implementation:
Comments:

CLOSING
Nothing moves in this world until someone sells something. It may not come as a surprise to you but any member of your staff who is in a customer facing position is in a sales role. However, the frightening part is that the people who are in these roles do not always see things this way.

One way of finding out whether any of your Service staff consider themselves to be in a sales role is to ask everyone to write down their own job description. The objective of this exercise is to see if anyone thinks that part of their job is "to sell hours".
There are a number of issues here that you might wish to consider. Firstly, if your people do not think that part of their job is to sell hours then quite simply they won't sell hours and so your first task is to enlighten your people so that they are aware that this is part of their job.

Secondly, sales training is not just for the vehicle sales team, it is for everyone who is in a sales role. Your people may be brilliant at giving advice and accurate quotations, but if they do not have the necessary selling skills to close the deal then all of their work will have been in vein. Find out which members of your team need help with their selling skills and find the appropriate sales training course that will best suit their needs. When you improve their selling skills they will sell more hours and your Productivity will increase.

Just remember that an opportunity to sell something is never lost, it's just found by someone else.

Date of Implementation:
Comments:

USE OF APPRENTICES
This is an operational area that causes distortion when you compare your statistics with others because many businesses account for their Apprentices in different ways, so here's a suggestion that might help with unification across the industry.

Before we decide on how to account for Apprentices, let's think about what we expect from them on an annual basis.

Year 1 Apprentices; in their first year do you expect an Apprentice to be productive? Most people's answer to this question is no. If this is the case, what are they doing in the first year? The answer is of course training and therefore their time and salary should be accounted for as training, which is an Indirect Expense. If you show their time as Hours Attended and Hours Worked there will be a distortion on both your Utilisation and your Productivity.

Year 2 Apprentices; do you expect them to be productive? Most people's answer here is 50%. In this case 50% of their time and 50% of their salary should be accounted for as training and the remaining 50% should be accounted for as Hours Attended with their salary being split between Labour Cost of Sales and Idle Time according to their levels of Utilisation and Productivity.

Year 3 Apprentices; do you expect them to be productive? Most people's answer here is 75%. In this case 25% of their time and 25% of their salary should be accounted for as training and the remaining 75% should be accounted for as Hours Attended with this portion of their salary being split between Labour Cost of Sales and Idle Time according to their levels of Utilisation and Productivity.

If you account for your Apprentices time and salary in this manner you will accurately identify their true abilities and you will also produce accurate measures for Utilisation, Productivity, Overall Efficiency, Labour Gross Profit, Idle Time and Direct Profit for the whole department. If you don't account for your Apprentices in this way _all_ of the above statistics will be distorted. The more accurate your Accountant can be with your figures, the better chance you have of increasing your performance because you cannot make a good decision with poor information.

These changes in costing apprentices are very easy to conduct and your Account only needs to make these changes once per year. If you do not account for your apprentices in this way your true Productivity will be hidden from view.

Date of Implementation:
Comments:

PICK'N MIX
Some jobs are easier to complete than others and that's why the mix of work that you do has a significant impact upon your Productivity.

For instance, if your workshop is loaded with mainly service schedules and PDIs, then you will complete those jobs quicker than the suggested book times and under these circumstances you can expect your Productivity to be reaching levels of around 125%. However, if your workshop is loaded with mainly repair and diagnostic work, the chances are that you will struggle to meet the book times because diagnosis is a difficult area to quantify because of differing technical skills between Technicians. Under these circumstances you can expect your Productivity to be reporting significantly lower.

When you are comparing your workshop Productivity with other dealerships you need to understand the mix of the work that is being undertaken because a workshop with high levels of service schedules will show much higher levels of Productivity than one with high levels of diagnosis work. Your mix of work is usually governed by two main factors:

1. Customer retention
2. Sales department activity

If you have a good customer retention programme then you will enjoy high levels of loyalty and a bias towards service schedules because your customers continue to return to you for all of their needs, not just repair items.

If your Sales department embarks in high levels of fleet activity you will have high levels of PDI work, which delivers high Productivity for your workshop, but low customer retention.

In summary then, you can influence your Productivity by understanding the mix of work that you load into your workshop. When you compare your Productivity with others you also need to compare your mix of work so that you gain a true reflection of this key area of performance. Analyse your own mix of work and notice when it changes and then compare how your Productivity changes with your mix of work.

Date of Implementation:
Comments:

JOB SELECTIVITY

Following on from the previous section, you can be selective with the type of work that you take on. For instance, if you take on a specialist task that you do not normally conduct then the chances are that your Productivity will suffer because you will not be familiar with the tasks involved. An option here might be to sub contract that specialist job out to another company so that your Productivity is protected. It is not always wise to take everything that is offered to you. One caveat here of course is that you have sufficient work to keep your workshop busy before you place work elsewhere.

Date of Implementation:
Comments:

COLLECTION AND DELIVERY

One of the main rules of the Service Department is never use productive staff for non-productive tasks. Collection and delivery is one of those tasks where Technicians are sometimes used but their time is not charged onto the customer. The solution is simple, charge your customers for collection and delivery.

Now before you discredit this idea think about the acres of diamonds story and don't make any assumptions <u>before</u> you try the idea. If you try this idea and your customers say no, you have lost nothing. If you charge your customers and they agree you will increase the Hours Sold and so increase your

Productivity and your bottom line profitability. Try this idea and then form your opinions, don't prejudge its value. Most importantly, do not use your Technicians for collection and delivery if you are not able to charge for their time.

Date of Implementation:
Comments:

GETTING STARTED
There are few Technicians who are eager to begin work first thing in the morning and getting them started in the right frame of mind can keep them motivated and productive for the rest of the day.

If a Technician has a difficult job or a job that he does not like at beginning of the day, he will spend more time thinking about how much he does not want to do that job before he even gets started. He may also look around the workshop and wonder why he's not been given an alternative job that is more to his liking.

One way of combating this negative mind set is try to allocate a good job first thing in the morning to get them started in the right frame of mind. Once the *easy* job has been completed the Technicians will be much more accepting of the more difficult tasks that are to follow in the rest of the day.

Date of Implementation:
Comments:

INCENTIVE PROGRAMMES

Here's a subject that is close to everyone's heart. Most bonus payments within a workshop are based upon Productivity, which means that Technicians get extra money for beating the allocated job times and these extra payments are often called time saved bonus. The question is, are these time saved bonus payments a good idea?

Firstly, if you put a bonus payment on any area of performance the likelihood is that you will improve that area so a time save bonus will improve your Productivity, BUT before you make any judgements, let's think about how this kind of programme actually works.

When you give a time saved bonus payment for beating the allocated job time you are actually rewarding your Technicians to reduce the number of Hours Worked. Let's take a look at how this type of system actually operates. *(In order to keep this example easy to understand, only one day is illustrated whereas in real life, all time saved bonus payments are usually awarded on a weekly or monthly Productivity result)*

(A) Hours Sold   = 8
(B) Hours Worked   = 8
(C) Productivity   = 100.00%   (A ÷ B x 100)
(D) Hours Attended = 8
(E) Hours Idle Time = 0

The example above shows Productivity at 100% and therefore no time saved bonus is awarded. Now look at what happens when Productivity increases by beating the allocated job times.

(A) Hours Sold   = 8
(B) Hours Worked   = 7
(C) Productivity   = 114.29%   (A ÷ B x 100)
(D) Hours Attended = 8
(D) Hours Idle Time= 1

In this scenario the Productivity has increased by the Technician completing the job in less time and the time saved bonus is now applicable. At this stage there are some important points for consideration.

Firstly, when you increase Productivity by reducing the number of Hours Worked you *automatically* create Idle Time and before you say "We put another job in that 1 hour that has been saved", it is important to understand that that issue is nothing at all to do with Productivity. Getting more work into the hour that has been saved is a question of increasing your Utilisation.

The second point is that the Hours Sold have not increased and therefore you have not generated any more revenue. In addition to this, you have paid a time saved bonus to your Technician which means that your costs have increased.

The main point here is that if your only bonus payments are based on beating the allocated job times you will automatically create more Idle Time and increase your wage costs. Beating the allocated job time is only half of the story because the real skill is to fill the time that has been saved with another job and unless all of your Technicians fully understand this principle you may not get full compliance if your incentive scheme is only based on time saved bonus.

However, if your Utilisation is well under control and you wish to continue with a Productivity based bonus scheme, here are some pointers for consideration.

How will your Productivity bonus scheme affect your quality control? There is a tendency to take shortcuts in procedures in order to earn bonus which will result in your customers needing to bring their vehicles back for rectification. This may have an impact upon your customer satisfaction index, which may result in a reduction in bonus payments from your manufacturer and a reduction in customer loyalty. Rectification charges or Policy cost are classed as an expense which you will find within your Indirect Expenses on your management accounts. Keep a regular check on your rectification costs to ensure that they are kept under control

Another consideration is the allocation of the bonus payment itself. Do you provide a team Productivity bonus where the whole of the department wins or loses the bonus, or do you provide an individual Productivity bonus for each Technician? Perhaps the safest bet is to provide a team bonus, but if you prefer an individual bonus then you must ensure that it is monitored closely to ensure fair play. For instance, if you have one Technician that is constantly higher than the others, you need to understand why this is happening. Is it because he receives favouritism and gets all the best jobs? Does he carry out his own rectification work, or is that given to an Apprentice to complete while he carries on with other tasks and therefore earns more bonus? Productivity bonus payments are fraught with loop holes and controversy and demand a great deal of control by the Service Manager, but it's merely a matter of preference.

So now the question is should we pay bonus on Utilisation instead of Productivity? The answer is no because this would swing the pendulum the other way and the Technicians would not be motivated to beat the allocated job times. So what are the options? Well, if you do intend to enrol your Technicians into an incentive programme, perhaps it is better to have the bonus payable on Overall Efficiency because they then have to maintain harmony and balance between Productivity and Utilisation then both the Technicians <u>and</u> your business will reap the rewards. By placing your incentive programme in this direction you are rewarding your Technicians to beat the allocated job times and then get onto another job as quickly as possible to fill the time they have saved with another job. This way, everybody wins because you will see the increase in revenue as your Hours Sold increase.

Date of Implementation:
Comments:

Menu Pricing

Most areas of Productivity are aimed at reducing the number of Hours Worked, but this initiative influences the number of Hours Sold.

Who decides how much time you should charge your customers to complete given tasks? Manufacturers produce book times for all tasks on their vehicles, but with the exception of Warranty work, these book times are only used as guidance.

It is both useful and comforting for your customers to see a price menu for many of the jobs that you do, just like when you go to a restaurant, you like to know how much things are going to cost you before you order them don't you?

Obviously you cannot possibly have a price menu for every job that you do so you need to be selective. However, who decides on the number of hours that you charge on each job on the menu? Here is an opportunity for you to review how many hours you are charging on each job. Unfortunately, when many Service Managers put together a price menu they have a tendency to undercut the manufacturers book times so that the prices look more competitive and this action causes two problems.

The first is that when you want to show a price reduction you should reduce your charge out rate and not the Hours Sold because the lower income will be shown in your recovery rate as it should be. If you reduce the Hours Sold you will reduce your Productivity and this will give you a false interpretation of your operational performance and the fact that a discount has been given will be masked.

The second problem is the mindset. Why would anyone want to charge fewer hours than the manufacturers recommended book times? Take a fresh look at your menu pricing and ensure that it is accurate and good value for money rather than cheap and you have the right number of hours to charge. If this action means that you have to increase some of your menu prices think of it this way: You can easily give a customer a discount if price is an issue for them, but you cannot ask them to pay you more money once you have published your prices.

Date of Implementation:
Comments:

CURRENT AVERAGES

In many cases Productivity is measured as a workshop average over the period of a month and most manufacturer's composites and IFCs show the monthly trend on a graph which is particularly useful. However, whilst the monthly workshop average is useful it does not illustrate where your strengths and weaknesses are in this area. For instance, you could have five Technicians where three of them are highly productive and two of them are not very productive and you could show an above average performance.

The way to get around this problem so that you know which of your Technicians are delivering high levels of Productivity is to measure their performance on an individual basis. You may be doing this already, but do you measure their current average?

If you measure individually on a monthly basis, you can have a Technician who does really well in his first few months and then his Productivity may decline but you will still think of him in his good days and rank him in line with these first months of production. The current average eliminates this problem so that you maintain a well balanced assessment of each Technician.

The current average is easy to apply and takes account of the peaks and troughs that occur on a monthly basis. All you need to do is to measure each Technician's Productivity on a monthly basis, and then to maintain the current average you simply calculate their Productivity again but this time using the last three months of figures rather than just one month.

Example:

Month	Hours Sold	Hours Worked	Productivity
Jan	190	160	118.75%
Feb	179	150	119.33%
March	180	189	95.24%
Current Average	**549**	**499**	**110.02%**

This example illustrates the Technician's average performance over the last three months of trading. The good thing here is that when you calculate next month's figures you keep a well balanced view of this Technician because the January figures will be discarded and the new April figures will be bought into the equation to maintain the current average.

Month	Hours Sold	Hours Worked	Productivity
Feb	179	150	119.33%
March	180	189	95.24%
April	184	172	106.98%
Current Average	**543**	**511**	**106.26%**

When you compare current average with the monthly performance you can clearly see the difference that this calculation makes in that you do not become influenced by simply comparing one month to the next. In order to maintain a respectable current average your Technicians will need to deliver good levels of Productivity on a consistent basis. In practice, when a Technician's current average begins to decline because they have a bad month they tend to put in extra effort in the following month to bring their performance back to a respectable level.

It's not what you do once in a while that delivers success; it's what you do on a <u>consistent</u> basis that delivers the results that you want and it is this current average that provides the measure of consistency.

Date of Implementation:
Comments:

CUSTOMER DIAGNOSIS

Fault diagnosis is a continuous problem when dealing with Productivity and proper diagnosis covers at least six individual areas of the process, the first of course is the initial meeting with your customer.

The main problem here is that most customers come to the dealership at the same time, which is usually first thing in the morning and the Receptionists are rushed off their feet trying to ensure that everyone is attended to before any problems arise. Of course this means that less time could be spent with each customer in obtaining all the information needed to identify the fault on the vehicle.

One possible solution here is to try to obtain more information over the telephone when the customer first contacts you and write that information down. When the customer then brings in their vehicle for repair ask them to go through the problem again and compare what they say with what you have written down from the telephone conversation because you will often get different information when they speak with you face-to-face. Remember that in this case, questions are the answer and the better you are at asking questions, the better the quality your answers will be.

In addition to this being a good cross reference check, it may also save you some time in the mornings when you have an overflow of customers waiting to see you. However, another alternative is to ask your customers to bring their vehicles to you at specific times rather than just saying bring your vehicle in first thing in the morning.

The main point here is that you need clarity of information from your customer otherwise your Technicians may spend unnecessary time trying to identify the problem rather than spending time fixing it.

Date of Implementation:
Comments:

TECHNICAL KNOWLEDGE FOR DIAGNOSIS
When you have gained all the information that you can from your customer, you may need to offer a diagnosis of the problem before you gain the work. In this case, does the person who qualifies your customers have sufficient technical knowledge in order to provide accurate fault diagnosis?

One of the problems that are caused here is that if an inaccurate diagnosis is given to the customer they will also probably have an inaccurate price to go with it. If the cost of the real fault is considerably more expensive you will have a dissatisfied customer and a problem on your hands, which may result in you having to reduce the number of hours in order to keep your customer happy. As a result, your Productivity will go spiralling downwards.

Check through a batch of your latest invoices and speak with your Service Receptionist to find out if this situation ever occurs. If it does occur, then it could be that your Receptionist does not have the right degree of technical expertise to conduct diagnosis and they will therefore require more specialist assistance from the workshop Foreman. However, when you do use your Foreman for non-productive tasks such as this you must ensure that he clocks off any productive work that he may be engaged with otherwise your Productivity will fall again.

This issue clearly demonstrates that Productivity is influenced in two very different ways. The Hours Worked are influenced by your Technicians and your Hours Sold are influenced by your front counter staff. You need to ensure that you are obtaining the correct information so that you make the right decision to improve your performance. You cannot make a good decision with bad information.

Date of Implementation:
Comments:

JOB CARD DESCRIPTIONS

OK, so now you are satisfied that all the right information has been gathered from your customers and an accurate diagnosis of the fault has been made. This stage now ascertains whether the Receptionist has put sufficient information on the job card so that the Foreman and Technician know what they are expected to do. If the Receptionist fails to communicate the faults effectively to the Technicians they will once again spend unnecessary time clocked onto the job and your Productivity will fall.

The way to ascertain whether your Receptionists are recording sufficient and correct information on the job cards is to take a random sample of job cards and examine them with this purpose in mind. It may mean more work for the Service Receptionists, but in the long run it creates much more profit for the company and much less frustration for the Technicians.

Date of Implementation:
Comments:

ACCURATE WRITE UP
Once the job card has been completed by the receptionist, it is now the job of the Technician to complete the work and return the job card to the Receptionist.

At this stage, it is critical that the Technicians provide an accurate write up, clearly identifying all work that has been conducted so that the correct number of hours can be charged to the customer. If the Technicians fail to list all of the jobs that have been conducted then some of those hours could be missed off the customers' invoices, which means that the Hours Sold will reduce and your Productivity will fall.

Here again take a random batch of the Technicians completed job reports and ensure that they contain sufficient information for the Receptionists to construct the invoices accurately. Once you are satisfied that the Technicians write ups reflect the quantity of the work that is being conducted it is worth while checking the write up procedure on a regular basis to ensure consistency.

Date of Implementation:
Comments:

TASK EXPANSION

When considering the subject of time management there is a popular theory that confirms that a task will always expand to fill the allotted time. This means that if you ask someone to complete a job within three hours that is how long they will take to complete the job. However, depending upon the job of course, in some cases it could have been completed in less time.

If you wish to improve your Productivity by experimenting with this philosophy yourself all that you have to do is give your Technicians an allocated time for a job that is fewer hours than you really expect. For instance, if you think a particular job should take 3 hours, tell your Technician that the allotted time is 2.5 hours and see what happens. Some people might say that you lie to your Technicians about the allocated job time and others might say that you are simply testing the limits. It's your call.

Date of Implementation:
Comments:

STORYBOARDING

Once you have all of your job card procedures in place how do you arrive at the number of hours to charge your customer? The price you charge does not need to be too cheap nor does it need to be too expensive, it's all about value for money or to be more precise, your "customers' perception" of value for money.

Your customers will be happy, providing that they perceive that they have value for money. If they think that you are "expensive" the likelihood is that they will complain when you present them with the bill and they will not return to you in the future or they will ask you to reduce amount of money payable.

The way that you invoice your work makes a big difference to how your customers perceive value for money. For instance, if you carry out a schedule A service for which your charge to the customer is 2.5 hours at £75 per hour your invoice could read as follows:

Invoice	
Carryout schedule A service	£187.50
Sub Total	£187.50
VAT @17.5%	£32.81
Total	£220.31

The problem here is that the customer does not know what work is involved in a schedule A service and therefore they will not know what work you have done on their vehicle so how do they form judgement on whether the £220.31 represents good value for money or whether it is expensive? You can guess right now which one of these they will choose.

The way to create value for money is to storyboard the invoice so that your customer can appreciate the amount of work that you have done for them. Let's say that a customer comes to you with a slipping clutch. You discover that the clutch needs replacing so you complete the job and present your customer with the invoice.

Standard Invoice	
Replace clutch as requested to include all genuine parts and labour	
Sub Total	£850.00
VAT @17.5%	£148.75
Total Payable	£998.75

The problem here is that the customer cannot assimilate what is involved in this job and therefore it may not represent good value for money so the idea of storyboarding is to inform your customer of exactly what work has been conducted on their vehicle so that they can understand and appreciate the cost involved. On the following page is a "real life" example provided by David Ashworth who is the Aftersales Manager of a truck dealership in the North of England.

Storyboard Invoice

1, Checked on reported clutch slipping, road test vehicle and confirm clutch slipping.
2, Position vehicle in workshop, jack up front end and support front axle on axle stands,
3, Disconnect battery,
4, Removed prop shaft bolts at gearbox end and centre bearing, and removed prop shaft, removed gear linkage, disconnected reverse light switch connection and disconnected tachograph cable. Clamped off hydraulic pipe and disconnected from union on bell housing, removed clutch release bearing from clutch pressure plate. Supported rear of engine and removed both gearbox mountings, placed transmission jack under gearbox and removed all bell housing bolts, removed the gearbox from the engine and lowered the transmission jack, checked the clutch release bearing for leaks found ok. Removed clutch cover and plate from flywheel and checked flywheel for damage, found to be ok, checked clutch, found to be worn, replaced clutch pressure plate and disc with new, fit new clutch assembly to flywheel, raised transmission jack and refit gearbox to engine, refit all gearbox mountings, reconnected reverse light switch, reconnected tachograph cable, reconnected hydraulic pipe to release bearing and bled hydraulic system. Refit prop shaft.
5, Re-connected Battery,
6, Jacked up front of vehicle and removed axle stands,
7, Carried out road test, all ok,
8, Re-checked all fluid levels, gear lever adjustment and all connections, all ok,
9, Took vehicle to tachograph station for tachograph cable re-seal.

	Sub Total	£850.00
	VAT @17.5%	£148.75
	Total Payable	£998.75

Now that you have seen two invoices for the same work and the same price, which of them do you believe would represent the best value for money?

By storyboarding your invoice in this way you give your customer a better understanding of what they are paying for and you will encounter far less resistance when you present your invoice for payment. In addition to this you will give away fewer discounts and it helps you to "sell" the value of the job when your Hours Sold deviates from the manufacturer's book times.

At first you might be thinking that this is a lot of effort to put into each invoice, but this task is not as difficult as you may think. Begin by building up a library of storyboards on computer for your most common invoices and over the next few months you can gradually add more examples to your collection and storyboarding will simply become an integral part of your invoicing procedures. All that you do is cut and paste onto your invoice and the process is effortless. If you are part of a dealer group you may find it useful to exchange your storyboards with colleagues so that you build up your library much quicker. When you adopt this storyboard strategy you will notice an immediate lift in your Productivity, create higher levels of customer satisfaction and also make more profit.

Date of Implementation:
Comments:

BOXED AND READY TO GO

When you hand the job card over to your Technician, it would be very helpful if you could also hand him everything else he needs to complete the job without any interruptions caused by having to collect parts. Pre-picking the parts is a practice that is very easy to apply particularly to routine service schedules. The question for you is when and how do you pre-pick the parts?

If you raise your job cards around two days in advance, you will generally know what parts have to be fitted with each job. When you liaise with the Parts Departments at this early stage they can gather the parts required and put them into a box ready to give to the Technician when he collects the job card and the Parts Department still have enough time to order the parts if they are not in stock. The parts can also be booked onto the job for invoicing ready for when the work is complete. This practice means that your Technicians do not spend any time going backwards and forwards to the parts counter waiting for parts which means that they will be able to complete the job in less time and so increase your productivity.

Date of Implementation:
Comments:

PARTS TRUE STOCK TURN

The availability of parts from stock is critical to maintaining good levels of Productivity. This does not mean that the parts department should keep huge amounts of stock, but it does mean that the stock that they do keep fits with the profile of work that you do. The best way to ascertain this fact is to liaise with your Parts Manager each month and keep track of the true stock turn in the part department because this will tell you how effectively the stock is being utilised. When the parts department have a good level of true stock turn they will also have low levels of parts ordered on VOR. This means that when your Technicians require parts, they are available from stock most of the time. If the parts true stock is low and there is a high volume of stock, the chances are that this will be bad news for you because a large amount of the stock will be moving into obsolescence rather than being useful in the workshop. If you are unable to obtain the parts that you require your Technician might have to stop working on the vehicle and put it all back together before he can begin with the next job. All of this means that you are working more hours on the vehicle which decreases your Productivity.

The benchmark for true stock turn varies between manufacturers because of the different stock order terms, but as a rule you should expect your true stock turn to be greater than 8 times per annum. If you or your Parts Manager are unfamiliar with true stock turn, please refer to The K.P.I. Book for further information.

Date of Implementation:
Comments:

DEVELOPING PARTS PROFILES

Does your Parts Manager keep the right profile of stock to service your workshop effectively, or do you have high levels of VOR?

The problem here is that if you motivate your Technicians to look for more work on each job and they begin selling up, that is all well and good, but if you do not have the parts in stock to fulfil those extra jobs your Technicians will think "why bother" and this will bring a very sharp and abrupt ending to your sell up strategy.

A solution to this problem is to keep a register of all of the parts that have not been available on the work that you sell up and give this register to your Parts Manager every week/month. By doing this your Parts Manager will know what parts are required for the future and you can continue with your sell up strategy.

Over a period of a few months you have a much more effective parts profile which means that you can sell more hours and complete those jobs in faster times which increases your Productivity.

Date of Implementation:
Comments:

LOCATION, LOCATION, LOCATION

This is just as true for the workshop parts counter as it is for your business. Have you considered the location of the parts counter that your Technicians use?

- Is it easily accessible?
- Is separate from customer facing areas?
- Is it separate from the service reception area?
- Is it in view of the workshop controller?
- Is it clear of all of the work bays?

All of these issues can have a positive or negative effect on your Productivity and all of them are worthy of your consideration.

Date of Implementation:
Comments:

RIGHT FIRST TIME

Improving your Productivity is all about achieving a balance between speed and quality. If you increase your speed and reduce the Hours Worked then your Productivity will increase, but if your Technicians cut corners and the quality of the work begins to suffer then you will be worse off than when you started because the customer will bring their vehicle back to you in order for it to be rectified.

When the vehicle is repaired this second time, the Hours Worked will increase, but you cannot charge your customer again for this work and so the Hours

Sold will remain the same and the result here is that your Productivity will decrease.

When customers bring their vehicles back to you for rectification, the cost of the Technicians time is borne by the Service Department and is shown as an Indirect or Semi-Fixed Expense called Policy Costs, Goodwill, or even Rectification. When you are able to get more jobs right first time you will have fewer rectification to deal with, your costs will decrease and your Productivity will increase so it's important to communicate to your Technicians that completing jobs quicker is the main target, but not at the expense of quality.

Date of Implementation:
Comments:

TEAM TECH
It is often said that teamwork always achieves more. Whilst it is not true for every situation on earth, it is an essential ingredient within your workshop. Imagine that you have a Technician that is working on a job that requires him lifting a heavy piece of equipment, probably too heavy for one man to manage. Where you have a good team spirit and everyone looks after each other, your Technicians will naturally help each other with these cumbersome tasks. However, your Productivity will tumble if you do not have a happy working environment where the Technicians are not supporting each other on such tasks. It is always worth your while observing the

relationships on the shop floor because it's not just your Productivity that is at stake, poor relationships lead to discontent, low levels of staff retention and more requests for pay rises! Are you aware of all of the relationships in your Service Department, and is there anything you can do to prevent animosity between your Technicians?

Date of Implementation:
Comments:

TIGHT REINS

Knowing who the boss is, respect, discipline, call it what you will, keeping control of everyone in the workshop is essential to keeping control of your Productivity, not to mention health and safety regulations and other such factors in your business. Some of the issues surrounding this area are smoking and mobile telephones. How often do the Technicians leave their work and gather together for a little chat whilst having a cigarette whilst they are still clocked onto a job? Do any of your Technicians make or receive telephone calls on their mobile telephones whilst still being clocked onto a job? Do you allow them to have mobile telephones in the workshop? What about the cleanliness of the workshop and the shop floor?

Legislation may protect you in the future on issues such as these, but what is happening now? You do not want to treat your Technicians like robots, but you do need to keep a tight rein on everything that happens.

Pride in their work, motivation and communication play a big part in this arena so ask yourself the question, how do you rate yourself in these areas and what can you do to make yourself better?

Date of Implementation:
Comments:

KEEP'EM TOPPED UP
It's usually the inexpensive and simple ideas that get overlooked because they appear to be insignificant at first glance, but they often yield great returns on your investment. This is one of those inexpensive simple ideas that significantly increased Productivity in a dealership in the South of England. The initial invest was just £1.50 in each work bay; Yes, you have read it correctly, just £1.50. Here's the story of what happened.

To begin with, each work bay was equipped with its own plastic watering can at a cost of £1.50 each. Over a period of time the watering cans became damaged as vehicles ran over them and other such little accidents happened until such was the time when there was only one watering can left in the entire workshop.

None of the Technicians had told the Service Manger that they no longer had a watering can at their work bay, they simply walked around the workshop to find the last remaining watering can. The search for the last watering can could have taken any amount of time and inevitably it was empty when they found it so the next trip was to the tap to fill it with water and then return to continue with the repair on the vehicle.

One day, the Service Manager noticed one of his Technicians wandering around the workshop, looking in all the corners and around each work bay so he asked the Technician what he was looking for. The Technician simply said "I'm looking for the watering can because I need to top up the levels." The Service Manager then said "Where is your own watering can?" The Technician replied "All of the other watering cans have been damaged so we've thrown them away and this is the only one that's left."

The Service Manager noted that it had taken eight minutes for the Technician to find the watering can and all of this time he was still clocked onto the job, which of course means that Productivity was falling.

The next day the Service Manager arrived for work with his arms laden with another load of watering cans, one for each work bay at a cost of £1.50 each. The net result was that Productivity increased significantly due to this minor investment, but after a short time, the watering cans were subject to accidents again and their numbers diminished.

The Service Manager in the South of England thought about this for a while and then decided that he would not buy any more watering cans because they would always be damaged and although the £1.50 investment was insignificant, he had a better idea.

He picked up the telephone and commissioned a Plumber to install the necessary pipe work so that each work bay had its own supply of water. The result was that the Technicians were no longer wandering around the workshop looking for the last remaining watering can and all of the jobs were being completed in faster times.

Is each of your work bays plumbed in to the water main, or are you still using watering cans? If you are still using watering cans just make sure that you have enough of them because the overall effect on your Productivity is astounding.

Date of Implementation:
Comments:

SPLIT SHIFTS
Do all of your Technicians turn up for work all at the same time, or do you split the shift by half an hour to have a staggered start and finish time?

The benefit of a staggered or split shift system is that you can get half of your team working on vehicles before the rest of the team arrive half an hour later, which means that they are not standing around waiting for jobs when they arrive for work. The gain in Productivity comes with the second shift getting started half an hour later. The later shift can see that the earlier shift is already working on vehicles and the "mind set" of getting started on the day's work becomes easier. The other gain is at the end of the day when the first team finish half an hour before the second team. The atmosphere changes and work speeds up because they want to go home.

In addition to these gains, the Receptionist has also had half an hour to get everything ready for the second shift in the morning, which means that if a customer is late or does not turn up, you have the time to reschedule the workload.

This idea works particularly well if you have eight or more Technicians working on the same shift pattern. You can also apply the same philosophy to lunch breaks too ensuring that your workshop is open over lunchtime when a customer comes in with an urgent problem. This gives you a lift in Productivity and more flexibility with workshop loading. When you adopt this idea, just make sure that you alternate the shifts or you will lose the psychological advantage.

Date of Implementation:
Comments:

NON FRANCHISE WORK

This is a double edged sword in that it can increase or decrease your Productivity depending on your experience and judgment. You may not have the necessary special tools for some jobs and therefore it may take longer to complete certain tasks and therefore decrease your Productivity. But on the other hand, because you may be unfamiliar with the vehicles, you might overestimate the job time and therefore increase your Productivity by completing the jobs quicker than you thought.

At the end of the day it's about remaining competitive in your marketplace and keeping the work flowing through your workshop. Non franchise work is all well and good but you need to be constantly aware of the mix and type of work that you are taking on so that you can maintain harmony and balance between income and your operational efficiencies. Assess your non franchise content and establish how *effective* you are with those vehicles taking all of these factors into consideration.

Date of Implementation:
Comments:

SELLING UP
When a customer books their vehicle in with you for a straightforward service schedule, what do you do? You could do exactly what the customer has asked you to do, no more, no less, or you could look for additional work that may be required.
The benefit of finding additional work is that you keep the work flowing smoothly, but there is a fine balance here because it is unwise to find additional work that is not justifiable; finding additional work must be conducted with honesty and integrity.
It is wise however, to identify any items that affect the safety of the vehicle, and done properly, your customer will appreciate your diligence and integrity.

Proving that you have an effective method for gaining authorisation from your customer to carry out the additional work, this avenue is well worth pursuing.

Selling up is a matter of habit and good practice for you and your customers. When a vehicle is booked in for a service, your customer might not be aware of any other faults that may exist. You owe it to your customer to thoroughly check the vehicle for them and you owe it to yourself and your business to optimise this opportunity.

Selling up increases the number of Hours Sold but the other gain in Productivity is that when you find this additional work, the vehicle is already stripped down and therefore the time taken to carry out the work will be reduced considerably, which means that the Technicians will easy beat the allocated job times.

You can assess whether your Technicians are finding this additional work by tracking the movement of your Parts Sales per Labour Hour. If they are finding additional work on standard serving schedules, your parts sales per labour hour will show an increasing trend.

Date of Implementation:
Comments:

VEHICLE JOCKEY
The vehicle jockey's job is to be a personal assistant to the Technicians and Receptionist. They locate keys and vehicles, load them into the work bays, collect

How To Improve Your Productivity

parts, organise consumables, collection and delivery; in short, they conduct all the non-productive duties, which allows the Technicians to continue working productively therefore completing work quicker than the allocated job times and so increasing Productivity.

The role of the vehicle jockey needs to be structured and he must only answer to one person otherwise the tendency is for this person to be used as an odd job man by other staff and you lose the advantage of increasing your Productivity.

When you calculate the cost of this additional person compare it to the additional hours that you could sell with all the extra time that you have freed up and remember to calculate the additional sold hours at your recovery rate. For example, let's say that your vehicle jockey will cost you £10 per hour and he will work for 40 hours per week, therefore the total cost is £400 per week. Now all you need to calculate is your breakeven volume, or in other words, how many additional hours will you need to sell in order to recover the cost of the vehicle jockey.

(A) Cost of Vehicle Jockey = £400 per week
(B) Recovery Rate = £75 per hour
(C) Breakeven volume = 5.33 Hours (A ÷ D)

This example shows that if your Recovery Rate is £75, you will need to sell an additional 5.33 hours per week to cover the cost of your vehicle jockey. Now put your own figures into the example and calculate the cost of a vehicle jockey for your business and then calculate how much more productive your workshop will be and realise the gains you will make in your profitability. You will see that it makes a significant increase to your business. If you are still not sure, why not begin with a part-time vehicle jockey to get you started with the process and control.

Date of Implementation:
Comments:

LOADING EFFICIENCY

You are reading this chapter because you are planning to improve your Productivity. Therefore if you are planning to improve your Productivity you should load your workshop accordingly. This might sound like a crazy statement to make, but some people just do not do this!

How do you measure your workshop loading? If you have 10 Technicians that clock-in for 8 hours per day, you have 80 Attended Hours that are available to you. The question is how many of those available hours do you book into the workshop each day?

Loading Efficiency is measuring the relationship between the hours booked into the workshop and the Hours Attended.

Example:
(A) Hours booked in w/shop = 88
(B) Hours Attended = 80
(C) Loading Efficiency = **110%** (A ÷ B x 100)

This example shows that there are more hours booked into the workshop than there are hours available to work. This relationship is significant because if your Productivity is greater than 100%, you will have time on your hands that will not be utilised.

Some people only load 90% of capacity "just in case" the additional time is required. You can usually see when this is happening because you tend to run out of work before the end of the day.

From a motivational standpoint, if there is not enough work booked in to the workshop, your Technicians will slow down. However, if they have to work faster to get the days work completed in time, the odds are that they will work faster and your Productivity will increase.

However, the main point here is that if you plan to increase your Productivity by beating the allocated job times, then you must load more work into the day to fill up the gaps that you are creating otherwise there is no point in increasing your Productivity because you will not gain anything. The point then is to plan to increase your Productivity by loading your workshop to more than 110%.

Date of Implementation:
Comments:

CREDIT CONTROL

A business can survive a long time without any profit but it cannot survive one day without any cash. Cash is the life-blood of all businesses and you are dependent upon its constant supply to keep your work flowing smoothly through the workshop.

Debtors are those people who owe you money and Creditors are those people to whom you owe money and generally speaking they should equate to the same value so that the money that you owe to your suppliers (Creditors) offsets the money that is owed to you by your customers (Debtors).

80% of businesses are foreclosed within their first 5 years of trading simply because they run out of cash and it's because all of their money is tied up in their customers' hands rather than being collected.

The average amount of time it takes your customers to pay you is called Debtors days. Ideally, you want your Debtor Days to be less than 45 days and if it is higher, this means that you are waiting longer to receive your money from your customers, which means that you have to invest more of your own money in your business to continue trading.

If you do not have this additional cash to invest in your business, it could mean that you encounter cash-flow problems and your suppliers may be difficult with you. This in turn could have a negative effect on your Productivity because if you are part way through repairing a vehicle and you need a part from a supplier that has your account on stop, the progress on the vehicle is halted, which means that you have to put it back together and start again when you have the parts available. Credit control is critical in all businesses because the availability of cash is the thing that allows you to continue trading. Here are some things to consider:

- Are your Debtor days around 45 days or less?
- Is your Work In progress under control and do you check it at least once a week?
- Do you ever have invoices sent back because they are incorrect?
- Do you have the correct invoicing procedures in place?
- Do you have good relationships with suppliers?
- Are your cash accounts actually paid in cash or do they go onto the debtors list?

Poor credit control is usually due to understaffing, fear of rejection or apathy, yet this is one of the most important aspects of any business. Some customers say that they will settle the bill with cash and then attempt to collect their vehicle and say that they will put a cheque in the post. One business that I work with has a rule that states that if any cash sales are not fully paid within 5 days, then no bonus will be paid to the Service Manager. You will not be surprised to learn that in their case, no cash sales find their way on to the Debtors list. As the old saying goes, Turnover is vanity, Profit is sanity, Cash is reality.

Date of Implementation:
Comments:

WORK IN PROGRESS

Work in progress (WIP) simply refers to the number of hours that have been booked onto jobs that have not yet been invoiced. In other words they are just like a Debtor because this represents money that is owed to you.

There are two factors concerning WIP that have an impact upon your Productivity with the first being the availability of cash. If you have completed the work but have not yet invoiced it, you have no way of getting paid for that work and you will have to put more money into your business to enable it to continue trading.

The second factor is that if the job has not yet been invoiced, then the Hours Sold will not be shown on your financial reports, but the time taken to complete the job, the Hours Worked, are taken into account therefore your Productivity will be reporting at a lower rate than you are actually achieving.

Many financial reports have a tendency to provide Work In Progress as a total monetary value, but this can often be misleading because you cannot be sure as to what it represents. You must ask the question, is it reporting a value based upon the Labour Cost of Sales, Hours Sold at retail value, or Hours Sold at the current Recovery Rate because some Accountants do this differently.

The most effective way to measure your Work In Progress is to ascertain how many days remain not invoiced because this may give you a clearer picture of what is happening.

Example:
(A) Hours booked as WIP = 120
(B) No of Technicians = 6
(C) Hours Attended in 1 day = 8 (Per Technician)
(D) **Work In Progress Days = 2.5 Days** (A ÷ B ÷ C)

The example above deals with the number of hours accumulated in Work In Progress and is therefore more useful for trend analysis. As a guideline, you should always maintain less than three days Work In Progress.

Date of Implementation:
Comments:

ACCESS TO TECHNICAL DATA

Where do you keep your reference manuals and computers for the access of technical data? The more time your Technicians spend searching for information or technical data the more time is being clocked onto the job and your Productivity of course diminishes.

An easy method of reducing this downtime is to erect proper shelving to house your technical manuals and to keep them maintained as you would a library. Make sure that your Technicians can gain access to them easily and they are maintained in an orderly fashion for future reference.

You can imagine what it would be like if you went to your local library to find some specific information and you found a pile of books in the corner of a room.

How much time would you spend looking through all of the books before you found the one that you need? Think of all that wasted time and also think about your mood and state of mind and how that would affect your work. It may take a little time to erect the shelving and properly categorise your manuals, but think about how often you will use them and how much time will be saved in the future. When you decide to adopt this idea, also adopt the idea of having a system for your Technicians to put them back in the right place when they have finished with them!

Date of Implementation:
Comments:

ASK YOUR TECHNICIANS

There are over 100 ideas in this book for improving your performance, but by far the best sources of information that you can tap into are the minds of your own Technicians. Again, this reinforces the point to make the most of, or to utilise the resources that you already have and that's why you'll find this same idea for improving your Utilisation.

Every productive on the shop floor has a wealth of ideas on how you can improve your workflow, but they won't tell you unless you ask them.
Don't assume that they know what you want. Some people don't like to give ideas because they don't want to be seen to be interfering. The idea of passing

on information may not even occur to some of your Technicians, and others may not want to come to you because their idea may be wrong and the fear of failure overrides their positive intent.

To overcome these problems you will have to communicate your wishes in the appropriate manner to suit each individual. For some people, a meeting where ideas can be shared and built upon will be ideal, but for others, a quiet chat now-and-again will better suit their level of confidence and contribution.

Other ideas that may work for you are to provide a suggestion box to capture ideas between meetings and also to provide rewards of some kind for the ideas that are successfully implemented.

However, before you go forward with any of these ideas, make sure that everyone fully understands Productivity by taking the time to explain what you are trying to achieve. When everyone knows what you are trying to achieve the feedback and ideas that you receive will be more valuable.

Date of Implementation:
Comments:

QUALITY ASSURED

So, your Technician has just completed a job within the allocated time and it now comes to the point of quality control but the question here is who conducts the quality control?

The Foreman plays a large role in this area of your Productivity but this is depending upon how his time is allocated. Although there are no hard and fast rules here, generally most Service Departments tend to book the Foreman as 50% Productive leaving him time to assist with other tasks, quality control being one of those tasks.

If the Foreman conducts all of the quality control for the workshop that leaves the Technician free to begin another job and the Hours Worked on that job are reduced and so Productivity increases. However, the downside to this strategy is that when a problem is encountered on the quality control the Technician then has to stop his new job and rectify the problem that has been found, which of course reduces your Productivity. This strategy highlights the importance of right first time. The questions to ask yourself here are:

- Who conducts your quality control?
- When a problem is encountered, what is the procedure?
- What level of Productivity do you expect your Foreman to achieve?
- Are problems that are found during quality control rectified by the Technician, the Foreman or an apprentice?

Date of Implementation:
Comments:

How Much Time?

To make any gains in Productivity you need to accurately identify and control the Hours Worked. This means that your Technicians must have some method for clocking onto a job when they begin and clocking off the job when it is complete. To improve Productivity, you need to increase the Hours Sold or reduce the Hours Worked, which means that you need accurately identify exactly what is happening otherwise you are blind to all activities.

At a more advanced level, your Technicians can clock on and off a job for specific reason such as waiting for parts or obtaining keys for a vehicle from the Sales Department; the amount of detail that you go into is really up to you, but the more effective you are at doing this practise, the higher your Productivity will be reported.

Let's get straight to the point. If you do not have a system in place for tracking how much time is spent on each job, get one right now, or forget all about any gains that you might be able to achieve with your Productivity. There are numerous systems on the market that enable you to track this time ranging from a simple clock card to barcodes and infrared guns. All of them are effective; it's just a matter of which one suits your particular needs.

Date of Implementation:
Comments:

WORKSHOP LAYOUT

The positioning of your work bays and all the special tools and equipment around them is critical to the flow of the work going through the workshop and the speed at which it can be completed.

In many cases, vehicles go in and out of the same door and this two-way traffic often causes disruption and congestion as some vehicles have to be moved in the busier times of the day. All of this additional vehicle movement is causing your Technicians to be clocked on their jobs for more hours and so decreases your Productivity.

Where it is possible, the best solution here is to have a one-way traffic system in operation so that vehicles come in through one door and go out through another door at the opposite end of the workshop. This prevents vehicles travelling in opposite directions in the same area of the workshop. If a one-way system is not possible for your current circumstances, you could still consider the layout of the workshop as a whole.

- Do vehicles have to be moved at anytime for other vehicles to gain access?

- Are the special tools and diagnostic equipment in easily accessible areas?

- Does the layout of your workshop help or hinder the flow of work?

- Are the work bays kept clean and tidy?

- Are waste bins emptied regularly, or are they overflowing with rubbish?

- Are all water and air hoses kept tidy or are they lying on the floor waiting for someone to trip over them?

- Are consumables easy to obtain?

- Are any of the work bays hindered by the Parts Counter or clock machine?

- Do your technicians have enough pride and motivation to keep their workshop clean and tidy?

Your focus of attention here is to clear the workshop of all obstacles and to consider if you need to change any aspect of the workshop layout that would speed up the job times.

Date of Implementation:
Comments:

PRE-AGREED AUTHORISATION LIMIT
When your customer leaves their vehicle with you for a service and you find additional work that requires authorisation, what do you do?

Well, of course you attempt to get in touch with your customer by calling the telephone numbers given, but your Technician could still be clocked onto the job and the clock is still ticking.

One solution to this problem is this: When you complete the diagnosis form with your customer, ask a question such as: "If we find any problems that affect the safety of your vehicle, naturally, they will need to be rectified. If it is going to cost a large amount of money, then we will contact you before doing any work, but if it is only a minor item, would you like us to rectify the problem for you so that your vehicle is safe?"

When your customer says "yes" you follow up with: "We'll be happy to do that for you. How much authorisation do you want to give us to complete such a task? Shall we say a maximum of £150?" *It is important to use a figure that is relevant and comfortable for you and the customer.*

When you have your customer's agreement, obtain a signature on your customer diagnosis form and if no additional work is necessary (here's the important bit) *make a point of telling your customer that you have not spent any of the authorised amount!* This will create feelings of trust in the mind of your customer, which is invaluable for repeat business.

If additional work is required, I still recommend that you attempt to contact the customer before you proceed, but if they are unavailable, you have the pre-agreed authorisation limit agreed so you can carry on with the job, workflow is not interrupted and non-productive time is avoided.

Date of Implementation:
Comments:

IF IT AIN'T BROKE, DON'T FIX IT

There have been many occasions where your Service Reception will have received telephone calls from customers asking for the cost of a certain repair ranging from a scheduled service to a clutch replacement. In some instances the enquiry could be a genuine question prior to them bringing their vehicle to you to have the work completed, but in some instances it could be that the customer is shopping around for the best price. This section is dealing with the latter; the price issue.

For the sake of an example, let's say that a customer calls your business on the telephone and asks you how much you are going to charge to supply and fit a new clutch. You must be aware at this stage that this could simply be a price enquiry and the customer will go to the business with cheapest price.

If you are a franchised dealership you may not be the cheapest, but you may be able to offer the best deal, especially with highly skilled franchise Technicians and genuine parts so your aim is to get face-to-face with the customer so that you can sell the benefits of your business.

Your first step is to resist giving a price over the telephone by making an irresistible offer to the customer such as, "Your clutch may not need replacing, it might only need adjusting. Why don't you bring your vehicle to us and we will have a look at it for you free of charge? You might be able to save some money that way. Would you like to bring it in this afternoon, or would tomorrow suit you better?"

Once the customer brings their vehicle into your workshop, you first drive it to make sure that the clutch is actually slipping and then you take it into the workshop to do the full assessment and during this time the customer is sitting in your comfortable reception area enjoying a nice hot drink.

Once you have completed the assessment, you can now go to the customer and say something such as, "Mr Jones, we've adjusted the clutch but it's still slipping. At least we tried to save some money for you. We now have your vehicle stripped down and unfortunately the clutch does need replacing. The total cost is £850, do you want us to go ahead and fix it for you?

Now you have the customer face-to-face and you are in the best position to overcome any price objections. You can talk about the franchise quality, skilled Technicians, genuine parts, warranty and all of the other benefits associated with your company and always end with an alternative close such as "Would you like us to take you home, and collect you when it's ready?" In most cases you will get the sale.

This is a great example of how your customer-facing staff should see part of their job as selling hours. When organised correctly, ideas such as this will improve both your Productivity and Utilisation and remember that nothing moves until somebody sells something.

Date of Implementation:
Comments:

HITTING THE RIGHT TARGET

When you decide to measure and monitor any area of performance whether it is Productivity or otherwise, you must keep everyone informed of what you are doing and why you are doing it. Whether you are implementing a bonus scheme or measuring the current average of each Technician you need to be absolutely specific and make sure that you give feedback to everyone who is connected with that area of performance. Remember that no one will go anywhere with you unless they know where you are taking them.

When you implement any of the ideas contained here you need to fully understand *how* they will affect your performance so that you can accurately convey your thoughts and ideas to your team. When you explain your aims, objectives and targets give some thought to everyone's motivation, not just your own. If you encounter any resistance to new ideas or targets, is it because you haven't explained your self well enough, or is it that you haven't given enough benefits? Before you go ahead with any ideas make sure that your team fully understands what you want and they area able to support your cause. When this is all in place ensure that you are measuring the right area of performance by continually checking the effects upon the Hours Sold and the Hours Worked because it is only these two factors that govern your Productivity.

Date of Implementation:
Comments:

IMPROVING YOUR PRODUCTIVITY
QUICK REFERENCE CHECK LIST

Bad Workmen And Their Tools ☐
Tool Diversity ☐
The Right Man For The Job ☐
Technical Training ☐
Commercial Training ☐
Closing ☐
Use Of Apprentices ☐
Pick'n Mix ☐
Job Selectivity ☐
Collection And Delivery ☐
Getting Started ☐
Incentive Programmes ☐
Menu Pricing ☐
Current Averages ☐
Customer Diagnosis ☐
Technical Knowledge For Diagnosis ☐
Job Card Descriptions ☐
Accurate Write Up ☐
Task Expansion ☐
Storyboarding ☐
Boxed And Ready To Go ☐
Parts True Stock Turn ☐
Developing Parts Profiles ☐
Location, Location, Location ☐
Right First Time ☐
Team Tech ☐
Tight Reins ☐
Keep'em Topped Up ☐
Split Shifts ☐
Non Franchise Work ☐
Selling Up ☐

Vehicle Jockey ☐
Loading Efficiency ☐
Credit Control ☐
Work In Progress ☐
Access To Technical Data ☐
Ask Your Technicians ☐
Quality Assured ☐
How Much Time? ☐
Workshop layout ☐
Pre-Agreed Authorisation Limit ☐
If It Ain't Broke, Don't Fix It ☐
Hitting The Right Target ☐

In some areas of performance there is a very thin line between Utilisation and Productivity, in fact you will have seen that there are one or two ideas that have been repeated in this book for improving both areas, however, although the ideas are the same, they affect your performance in a slightly different ways. Not all ideas have been repeated so it is now your challenge to identify which of the actions and ideas can have a positive impact upon both Utilisation and Productivity because it is those ideas that will bring you the biggest reward in the shortest amount of time.

To meet this challenge you will need to read every idea and fully understand how the actions will affect the Hours Sold, Hours Worked and Hours Attended and then interpret what effect that those changes will have on your operational performance. All the information you need to rise to this challenge is contained within this book; you must continue prospecting for your own acres of diamonds and remember to revisit these ideas at regular intervals; don't try to do everything at the same time.

To conclude this chapter I'll leave you with one final thought. You may have some of these ideas already in place in your business but are you achieving your full potential in all of them or can you revisit them and do even better?

We are what we repeatedly do.
excellence then, is not an act, but a habit

- Aristotle

PART III

HOW TO CALCULATE THE GAIN IN YOUR OPERATIONAL EFFICIENCIES

Chapter VII

Calculating The Gain In Your Utilisation

*"If people only knew how
hard I work to gain my mastery,
it wouldn't seem so wonderful at all."*

- Michelangelo

Chapter VII

Calculating The Gain In Your Utilisation

Utilisation is the relationship between Hours Worked and Hours Attended. The Hours Worked are influenced by good Service Management and the Hours Attended are influenced by the number of Technicians you employ and the amount of overtime that you allow. Therefore when you plan to improve your Utilisation you need to understand by what method you are going to achieve the increase because the effects upon your profitability are very different. This chapter will show how to calculate improvement in the Hours Worked because that is where the real gains in profitability are made.

Let's examine the words of Michelangelo contained within the opening quotation. My own interpretation of his words is this: "The quality of your results is determined by the quality of your preparation". You must spend time preparing and you must fully understand a subject before you can deliver the results that you first set out to achieve. No prizes for guessing what happens when you fail to prepare. Before you embark on your journey of improving Utilisation, you first have to know what you want to achieve. You would not expect the captain of a ship to set sail into an ocean without a chart and course and hope to end up in the port of his choice. He has to plan the journey well in advance; even before he steps aboard the ship.

If you think about it for a moment, you follow exactly the same principle every time you get into your car. First you decide where you want to go and then you get in your car and go there. If you don't know the way to your destination you will either ask someone, look it up on a roadmap or rely upon your satellite navigation system. Whichever method you choose, you will want to know how to get there *before* you begin your journey. This same philosophy also applies to improving your Utilisation. Firstly, you must prepare the road ahead and you can then make sure that the actions you are taking are moving you in the right direction.

GETTING IT RIGHT FROM THE BEGINNING
Utilisation is measuring how much of your attended time is spent working productively. To begin exploiting this profit opportunity you must be able to separate your Technicians Hours Worked from their Idle Time. In its most basic form, this means that your Technicians must clock on and off each job and if you do not follow this practice you will not be able to realise all of the profit that is rightfully yours. Here's a quick reminder of the time categories that you need to capture:

Hours Attended = Number of hours that your Technicians have been on-site and available to work.

Hours Worked = Number of hours that your Technicians have been clocked onto jobs.

Idle Time = Number of hours that your Technicians have attended, but have not been *not* been clocked onto jobs.

WHERE ARE YOU NOW?

Calculating Utilisation from your results is very easy and if you are fortunate, your management accounts may already have this key performance indicator present. However, if you need to calculate your result manually here's a quick reminder:

(A) Hours Worked = 1,042
(B) Hours Attended = 1,226
(C) Utilisation = 85% (A ÷ B x 100)

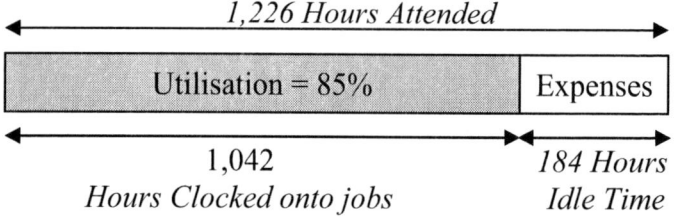

```
←――――――― 1,226 Hours Attended ―――――――→
┌─────────────────────────────────┬──────────┐
│       Utilisation = 85%         │ Expenses │
└─────────────────────────────────┴──────────┘
←――――――――――――――――――――――→ ←――――→
          1,042                      184 Hours
    Hours Clocked onto jobs          Idle Time
```

In this example you can see that the Technicians have attended 1,226 hours and have been clocked onto jobs for 1,042 hours, which means that they have been utilised for 85% of the attended time.

Idle Time represents the amount of attended time that has <u>not</u> been clocked onto jobs and therefore the calculation for Idle Time is your Hours Attended minus your Hours Worked. Utilisation is all about reducing Idle Time by working more of the Hours Attended.

WHERE DO YOU WANT TO BE?

Firstly, you need to decide the level of increase you think that you can achieve with Utilisation and then you can forecast how much more profit you can make from the actions you are considering.

Calculating The Gain In Your Utilisation

There is no point implementing actions if they are not going to deliver enough profit so it is best to calculate the amount of profit you will make *before* you implement your actions.

When you increase Utilisation a number of things will change such as Hours Worked, Hours Sold, Labour Sales, and let's not forget about the increases in your profit. The question is how do you calculate these changes so that you know what is going to happen well in advance?

Utilisation can be increased by either increasing the Hours Worked or reducing the Hours Attended. Because this chapter is about business growth the area of focus is placed upon increasing the Hours Worked with more jobs going through the workshop rather than reducing the Hours Attended.

In any event, Utilisation is based upon the number of Hours Attended and therefore the steps that you follow to recalculate the improvements in Utilisation are the same because they are always based upon the number of Hours Attended. This means that when you make any changes in your Utilisation the steps needed to calculate the changes in performance are exactly the same. With this in mind, let's begin the process of understanding how the changes in your operational performance are shown on your financial reports and management accounts.

When you look at a whole page of figures they can be daunting at first sight, so this simple 7-step system makes the whole planning process easy to understand.

7 STEPS TO CALCULATING IMPROVEMENT

To get started let's create a small business called Insight Motors and use their statistics as a working example. When you understand the process for yourself you can replace the figures with your own.

Utilisation for Insight Motors:

(A) Hours Worked = 1,870
(B) Hours Attended = 2,200
(C) **Utilisation** = **85%** (A ÷ B x 100)
(D) Hours Idle Time = 330 (B – A)

The benchmark for Utilisation is 85% to 95%, which means that Insight Motors certainly have plenty of room for improvement. Now let's use the 7 easy steps to realising more profit from Utilisation.

STEP 1: INCREASE HOURS WORKED

Utilisation at 85% is too low so for the purpose of this exercise, let's make a decision to set a target of 91%, which is an increase in Utilisation of 6%. Now that you know what you want to achieve, you can begin with your process of improvement. As you will see, it's not simply a matter of increasing your profit by 6% because other things change too.

When you increase Utilisation, your Hours Attended remain constant, but you increase the number of Hours Worked because you will be putting more jobs through the workshop and therefore working more of the attended time. All that you need to do here is take the Hours Attended and multiply this figure by your target Utilisation to obtain the improved Hours Worked:

Calculating The Gain In Your Utilisation

	Current		Improved
(A) Hours Attended	= 2,200		2,200
(B) Utilisation	= 85%		91%
(C) Hours Worked	= 1,870	(A x B)	2,002
(D) Hours Idle Time	= 330	(A - C)	198

Here you can see that Hours Attended remains constant, but the Hours Worked increases to reflect the 6% improvement in Utilisation. As a result of the Technicians working on more jobs, you can also see that you have much less Idle Time.

Now that there are more jobs going through the workshop there will be an increase in the Hours Sold, but the question is how many more hours will you sell?

STEP 2: INCREASE HOURS SOLD

To calculate how many more hours you will sell as a result of the improvement in Utilisation you simply multiply the number of Hours Worked by the rate of your Productivity. To understand the full impact of Utilisation, let's assume that Productivity remains constant throughout this exercise so that there are no distortions. For this example, let's say that Insight Motors are reporting their Productivity at 112% therefore the increase in Hours Sold is calculated as follows:

Hours Worked x Productivity = Hours Sold

		Current	Improved
Hours Worked	=	1,870	2,002
Productivity	=	112%	112%
Hours Sold	=	2,094.40	2,242.24

Here you can see that the Hours Sold has increased by 147.84 hours. Remember that this has been made possible by getting more jobs through the workshop and not by working any faster. Insight Motors have *utilised* more of the attended time and as a direct result of this the Idle Time is also reduced as you can see below.

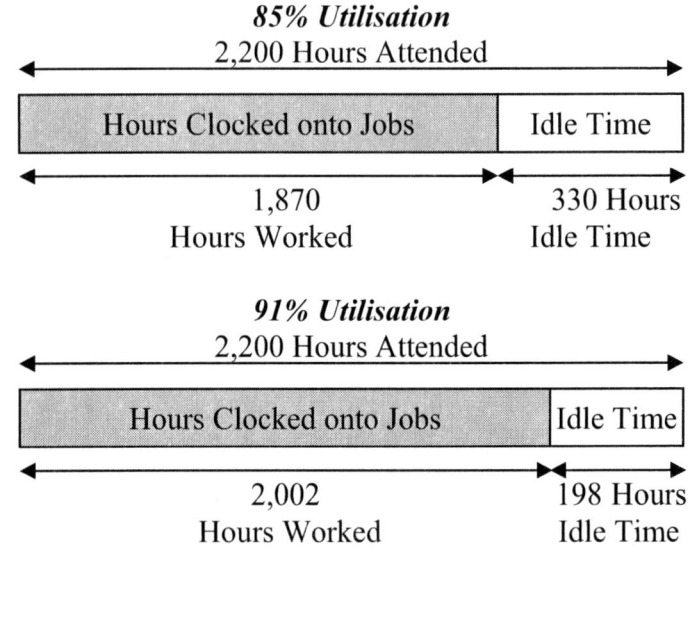

85% Utilisation
2,200 Hours Attended

| Hours Clocked onto Jobs | Idle Time |

1,870 Hours Worked — 330 Hours Idle Time

91% Utilisation
2,200 Hours Attended

| Hours Clocked onto Jobs | Idle Time |

2,002 Hours Worked — 198 Hours Idle Time

	Current	Improved
Hours Sold	2,094.40	2,242.24
Hours Attended	2,200	2,200
Hours Worked	1,870	2,002
Hours Idle Time	**330** ⇨	**198**

In completing steps 1 and 2 you have established all of the changes in the various types of hours that have been bought about by the increase in Utilisation. Please ensure that you fully understand how these figures have been calculated before you continue.

STEP 3: INCREASE LABOUR SALES

Now that you have increased the Hours Sold, how much revenue are they worth to you? To answer this question, you need to establish the value of Labour Sales which is calculated by taking the number of Hours Sold and multiplying them by your Labour Recovery Rate.

Take care here; the increase is not to be calculated by using your Charge Out rate because discounts are often given and this would give you an overstated Labour Sales figure. Your Recovery Rate is the figure to use here because this is the figure *after* discounts have been given.

Ideally, you would use the Hours Sold and the Recovery Rate for each income sector such as retail, warranty and internal to give you a more accurate and meaningful figure as in the example below.

	Hrs. Sold	Recovery Rate
Retail	1050	£69.20
Warranty	160	£57.48
Internal	290	£67.50

For the sake of simplicity, the following model uses the Total Hours Sold and the average Recovery Rate, so that you can see the calculations more easily. Keep in mind that your Retail Recovery Rate is probably a lot higher than your Warranty Recovery Rate, which again will be different to your Internal Recovery Rate and you will have different volumes of work going through each sector which distorts the average even further. Where possible split your Recovery Rates as shown above for a more accurate figure.

In this example, Insight Motors are reporting their Average Labour Recovery Rate at £64.56 so the increase in Labour Sales can now be calculated as follows:

Hours Sold x Recovery Rate = Labour Sales

	Current	Improved
Hours Sold	2,094.40	2,242.24
Recovery Rate	£64.56	£64.56
Labour Sales	**£135,214.46** ⇨	**£144,759.01**

Here you can see the additional revenue that has been generated from the increased number of Hours Sold equates to an increase of £9,544.55.

Naturally, you will also make more profit from Oil Sales, Sub Let and any other services that you offer, but for the sake of simplicity, these items have been omitted so that you can see the effects of Utilisation in isolation. However, now that you have increased the Hours Sold and Labour Sales, how much money has it cost you to complete this task?

STEP 4: INCREASE LABOUR COST OF SALES

To calculate how much the increases have cost you, you need to calculate your Labour Cost of Sales. This is the part of the Service Department that causes the most confusion so take care here. *The Labour Cost of Sales refers only to the Hours Worked and not the Hours Attended.* The cost of any attended time that has not been worked is classified as Idle Time and is shown within your expenses.

Calculating The Gain In Your Utilisation

The Labour Cost of Sales is calculated by taking the number of Hours Worked and multiplying this figure by the average amount of money that you pay your Technicians per hour. The money paid to your Technicians is called the Average Labour Cost.

Insight Motors are reporting their Average Labour Cost at £12.95 per hour. This is the average amount of money paid to each Technician per hour. Now that you have this figure, you can re-calculate the Labour Cost of Sales as follows:

Hrs Wkd. x Av. Lab. Rate = Lab. Cost of Sales

	Current	Improved
Hours Worked	1,870	2,002
Av. Labour Cost	£12.95	£12.95
Labour Cost of Sales	**£24,216.50**	**£25,925.90**

Here you can see that the Labour Cost of Sales has increased by £1,709.40 but keep in mind that the Idle Time will reduce by £1,709.40 *because the money that you pay your Technicians to attend your business is split between Hours Worked and Idle Time.*

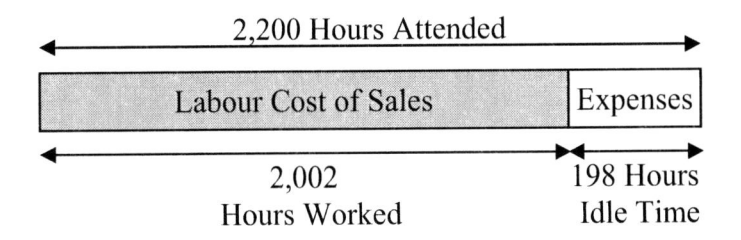

```
         2,200 Hours Attended
◄─────────────────────────────────►
┌─────────────────────────┬───────┐
│   Labour Cost of Sales  │Expenses│
└─────────────────────────┴───────┘
◄─────────────────────────►◄──────►
         2,002              198 Hours
       Hours Worked         Idle Time
```

Now you can see that the "real cost" of increasing your Utilisation is zero because you have to pay your Technicians for the Hours Attended whether they are working or not, but it is very important to show the costs in the right places otherwise you could make some false conclusions about your business.

If your Accountant does not split the Technicians salary between Labour Cost of Sales and Idle Time, you will not be able to see how much of your time is being utilised and you will therefore be blind to any improvement that could be made. If your Technicians total salary is placed within the Labour Cost of Sales then your Labour Gross Profit will be adversely reduced and this again could lead you to make some false assumptions about your business, so ensure that your information is correct before you make any changes in operational performance.

Now that you have completed 4 steps, you have the following information in place:

	Current	Improved
Hours Sold	2,094.40	2,242.24
Hours Attended	2,200	2,200
Hours Worked	1,870	2,002
Hours Idle Time	330	198
Recovery Rate	£64.56	£64.56
Av. Labour Cost	£12.95	£12.95
Labour Sales	£135,214.46	£144,759.01
Cost of Sales	£24,216.50	£25,925.90

Please carefully review these figures and ensure that you fully understand the logic contained within each step before you continue reading.

Step 5: Calculate Labour Gross Profit

At this stage of the process you have increased the Hours Worked, increased the Hours Sold, increased Labour Sales and increased Labour Cost of Sales, and now you want to know how much profit you have made in the process?

Profit is measured at two different points within all businesses and the first profit measurement is called Gross Profit.

The term "Gross" literally means "without deduction" therefore calculating the Gross Profit of any product is simply Sales minus Cost of Sales *before* any expenses are taken into account. Because Idle Time is an expense, now you can see why it is so important to exclude it from the Labour Cost of Sales.

In this example, you are only measuring the effects upon Labour Gross Profit and so the formula is simply:

Labour Sales minus Labour Cost of Sales.

	Current	Improved
Labour Sales	£135,214.46	£144,759.01
Cost of Sales	£24,216.50	£25,925.90
Labour G.P.	**£110,997.96** ⇨	**£118,833.11**

Now you can see that the Labour Gross Profit has increased by £7,835.15 in monetary terms, a great result. However, to understand what has happened to your business real terms you need to calculate the Labour Gross Profit % which is calculated as follows:

Labour GP ÷ Labour Sales x 100 = Labour GP%

	Current	Improved
Labour Sales	£135,214.46	£144,759.01
Cost of Sales	£24,216.50	£25,925.90
Labour G.P.	£110,997.96	£118,833.11
Labour G.P. %	**82.09%** ⇨	**82.09%**

However, it is interesting to note that the Labour Gross Profit % has remained constant at 82.09% even though the *value* of the Labour Gross Profit has increased. This is critical point to understand.

The Labour Gross Profit % has remained constant because the Labour Sales and the Labour Cost of Sales have increased at the same rate and therefore the relationship between them must also remain the same. As the Sales increase, so does the cost of sales. Now you can see the importance of calculating the Labour Cost of Sales correctly because ***Utilisation does not affect your Labour Gross Profit %***.

Now you know that if you want to influence your Labour Gross Profit %, Utilisation will not provide the answers that you require, although it significantly increases the amount of Labour Gross Profit that you make. Labour Gross Profit and Labour Gross Profit % are two completely different things.

The baseline for Labour Gross Profit is to be greater than 75%, but before you make any judgements on this figure, first make sure that your Accountant is putting your figures in the right places on your management accounts or you could be drawn into making wrong decisions about your profitability.

The most common error that Accountants make is to put the total cost of the Technicians salary as the Labour Cost of Sales. Typically, this can also include holiday, sickness and training. Many Accountants do this because they do not fully understand the Service Department and it is an easy accounting practice to conduct. However, this is a very dangerous practice because you cannot see what is happening in your business! To be in control of your department, you have to know where your money is being used effectively and where it is not being used effectively and your Technicians salary is no exception. Your Technicians salary is in fact located within three different places; here is how your accounts should be structured in order to interpret your operational performance correctly:

- Labour Cost of Sales represents the money paid to Technicians for the Hours Worked, or the hours clocked onto jobs whilst they are attending. Any productivity bonuses paid to Technicians should also be included here, but be careful with Overtime because you should only capture the time clocked onto jobs.

- Idle Time represents the money paid to Technicians whilst they are attending, but *not* clocked onto jobs, including Overtime. This is found within your Direct Expenses, *not* your Labour Cost of Sales.

- The money that you pay your technicians for Holiday, Sickness and Training is to be found within your In-Direct Expenses.

At this stage of your 7-step process you have calculated everything up to the point of Labour Gross Profit, but have you incurred any expenses along the way?

STEP 6: CALCULATE EXPENSES

Within a department there are two types of expenses; those triggered by sales volume and those that are not triggered by sales volume. Direct Expenses are only accumulated when you sell something and In-Direct Expenses are evident whether you sell anything or not.

For the purposes of this illustration only Idle Time will be separated from all other expenses so that you can clearly see the effects of Utilisation because most other expenses (apart from Consumables) will remain constant. The cost of Idle Time is calculated by taking the number of Hours Idle multiplied by Average Labour Cost. In this working example for Insight Motors, the number of Hours Idle will be reduced because Utilisation has been increased resulting in more hours being worked. You may recall that you calculated this change in Idle Time in Step 2 and the Average Labour Cost for Insight Motors was given in Step 4.

Hours Idle x Av. Labour Cost = Cost of Idle Time

	Current		Improved
Hours Idle Time	330		198
Av. Labour Cost	£12.95		£12.95
Cost of Idle Time	**£4,273.50**	⇨	**£2,564.10**

Calculating The Gain In Your Utilisation

Here you can see that the cost of Idle Time has reduced by £1,709.40. If you now look back to Step 4, you will see that the Labour Cost of Sales increased by £1,709.40 which is exactly the same amount. This is because you still have to pay your Technicians to attend your business whether they are working or not, but the money you pay them is split between Hours Worked and Idle Time.

The Hours Worked captures the amount of money you have paid your Technicians whilst they *have* been clocked onto jobs, and the Idle Time captures the amount of money you have paid your Technicians whilst they *have not* been clocked on to jobs. In simple terms, the more hours they spend clocked onto jobs the lower your Idle Time; the fewer hours they spend clocked onto jobs, the more your Idle Time. When you add Idle Time and Hours Worked together you will come up with your Hours Attended.

At this stage of the process you have completed six of the seven steps. You have increased the Hours Worked, increased the Hours Sold, increased Labour Sales, increased Labour Cost of Sales, increased Labour Gross Profit, decreased Expenses and now comes the seventh step and moment of truth. How much profit has been delivered to the bottom line and is it therefore worth making the effort to increase Utilisation?

STEP 7: CALCULATE DEPARTMENTAL PROFIT

Departmental Profit is the final calculation in the accounting process for the Service Department and it is also known as the bottom line, Operating Profit or Direct Profit.

If Gross Profit is the calculation *before* Expenses have been taken into account, then Departmental Profit is the calculation *after* Expenses have been taken into account. The formula for Departmental Profit is simply:

Gross Profit minus all Departmental Expenses

	Current	Improved
Labour G.P.	£110,997.96	£118,833.11
Dept. Expenses	£71,520.17	£69,810.77
Dept. Profit	**£39,477.79** ⇨	**£49,022.34**

Here you can see that the Departmental Profit has increased by £9,544.55 and it has not been eaten away by expenses; an excellent way to grow your business. But now you need to know if it has been increased in real terms, or in other words, has the Departmental Profit increased as a percentage, or have we been busy fools?

Departmental Profit ÷ Labour Sales Value x 100

	Current	Improved
Labour G.P.	£110,997.96	£118,833.11
Dept. Expenses	£71,520.17	£69,810.77
Dept. Profit	£39,477.79	£49,022.34
Dept. Profit %	**35.57%** ⇨	**41.25%**

Success! Departmental Profit% has increased from 35.57% to 41.25%, which clearly demonstrates sound business growth. This is great news, but don't get carried away just yet because here is a very important point to understand. You will recall from Step 5 that the Labour Gross Profit % remains constant, but here the Departmental Profit % is showing an increase of 5.68%. Now you can see the real value in increasing Utilisation because the extra profit that is generated goes straight to your bottom line. Utilisation is the biggest profit builder within the Service Department because your bottom line profits increase and your expenses reduce.

In conclusion, when you improve your Utilisation by increasing the number of Hours Worked and reducing Idle Time you will see the effects of your work in the following areas on your management accounts:

Summary of Effects

Hours Attended	⇨	**No Change**
Hours Sold	⇨	**Increase**
Hours Worked	⇨	**Increase**
Productivity	⇨	**No Change**
Utilisation	⇨	**Increase**
Overall Efficiency	⇨	**Increase**
Labour Sales	⇨	**Increase**
Cost of Sales	⇨	**Increase**
Labour G.P.	⇨	**Increase**
Labour GP%	⇨	**No Change**
Expenses	⇨	**Reduce**
Dept. Profit	⇨	**Increase**
Dept. Profit %	⇨	**Increase**

On the following page you can see how these changes in operational performance are shown within the Law of the Service Department.

Before the change in operational performance

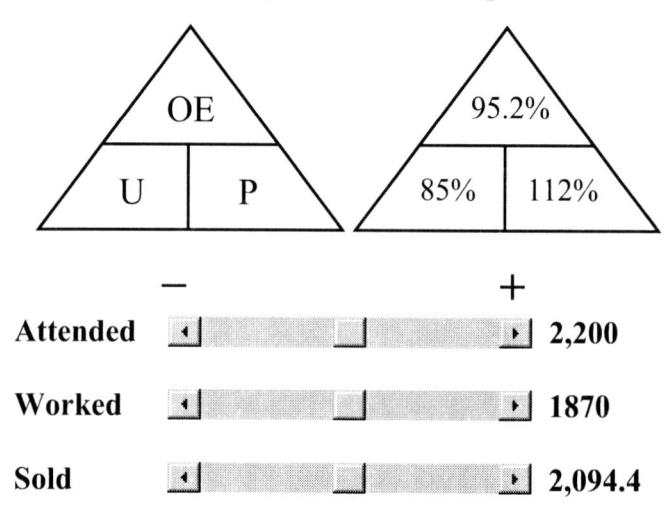

- OE
- U | P

- 95.2%
- 85% | 112%

	−	+
Attended		2,200
Worked		1870
Sold		2,094.4

After the change in operational performance

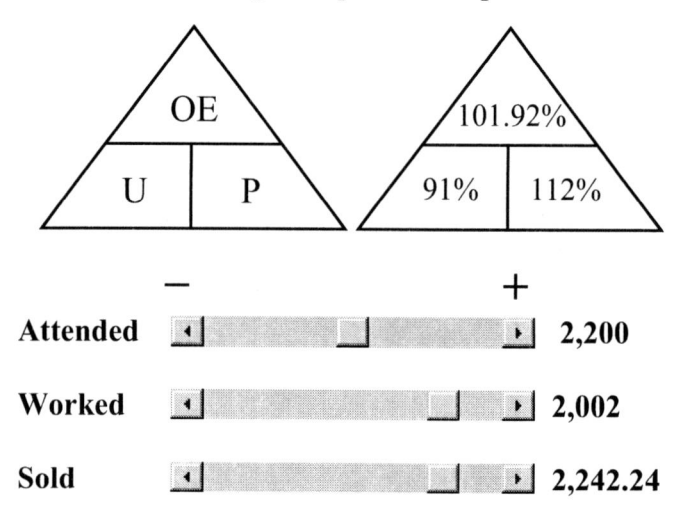

- OE
- U | P

- 101.92%
- 91% | 112%

	−	+
Attended		2,200
Worked		2,002
Sold		2,242.24

Remember that these gains are produced by getting more jobs through the workshop in the same amount of available time.

THE DOWNSIDE

The previous example has shown the positive effects of increasing your Utilisation by loading more jobs into the workshop and completing those within the same time available. In other words it's an example of what happens when you make more use of your resources. However, it is possible to increase your Utilisation without achieving any gain at all. If your Technicians do not use the clock to properly identify non-productive time then it could be that Idle Time will not be shown. Remember that Hours Worked are common to Utilisation and Productivity and if your Technicians do not show Idle Time then your Utilisation will be Overstated and your Productivity will be understated and there will be no change in your Overall Efficiency as shown below.

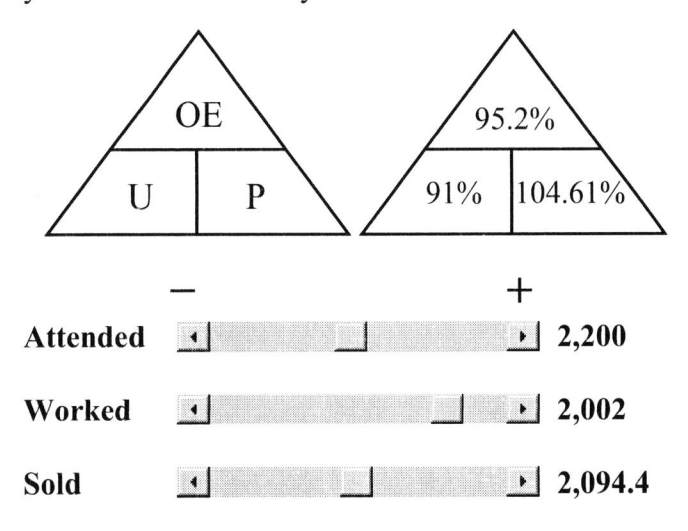

```
        /\                    /\
       /OE\                  /95.2%\
      /----\                /--------\
     / U  P \              / 91% |104.61% \
    /--------\            /----------------\
```

     —   +

Attended ◄▬▬▬▬▬▬▬▬▬▬► 2,200

Worked ◄▬▬▬▬▬▬▬▬▬▬► 2,002

Sold ◄▬▬▬▬▬▬▬▬▬▬► 2,094.4

When you increase your Utilisation you need to ensure that you are increasing the Hours Worked by loading more jobs into the workshop and not just remaining clocked onto the *same* jobs.

The 7 Steps In View

1. **Calculate Hours Worked**
   Hours Attended x Utilisation %

2. **Calculate Hours Sold**
   Hours Worked x Productivity %

3. **Calculate Labour Sales**
   Hours Sold x Recovery Rate

4. **Calculate Labour Cost of Sales**
   Hours Worked x Average Labour Cost

5. **Calculate Labour Gross Profit**
   Labour Sales minus Labour Cost of Sales
   Labour GP % = Labour GP ÷ Total Sales x 100

6. **Calculate Expenses**
   Hours Idle x Average Labour Cost

7. **Calculate Departmental Profit**
   Gross Profit minus Departmental Expenses
   Dept. GP % = Dept. GP ÷ Total Sales x 100

Now calculate the whole process for yourself on the following page or if you prefer to keep your book nice and clean you can download the page from www.askinsight.com/service96

Fill In The Blanks

(A) Hours Sold   =
(B) Hours Attended   =   2,200.00
(C) Hours Worked   =
(D) Hours Idle Time   =

(E) Recovery Rate   =   £64.56

(F) N° of Technicians =   10
(G) Average Labour Cost = £12.95

(H) Labour Sales   =
(I) Labour Cost of Sales =
(J) Labour Gross Profit =
(K) Gross Profit %   =

(L) Cost of Idle Time =
(M) All Other Expenses =   £67,246.67
(N) Department Expenses =

(O) Department Profit =
(P) Department Profit % =

(Q) Utilisation   =   85.00%
(R) Productivity   =   112.00%
(S) Overall Efficiency =   95.20%

When you have finished this exercise, you can check out your answers on the following page and you can see the differences with the increase in Utilisation.

Insight Motors Report for 1 Month

(A) Hours Sold = 2,094.40
(B) Hours Attended = 2,200.00
(C) Hours Worked = 1,870.00
(D) Hours Idle Time = 330.00   (B - C)

(E) Recovery Rate = £64.56

(F) N° of Technicians = 10
(G) Average Labour Cost = £12.95

(H) Labour Sales = £135,214.46   (A x E)
(I) Labour Cost of Sales = £24,216.50   (C x G)
(J) Labour Gross Profit = £110,997.96   (H - I)
(K) Gross Profit % = 82.09%   (J ÷ H x 100)

(L) Cost of Idle Time = £4,273.50   (D x G)
(M) All Other Expenses = £67,246.67
(N) Department Expenses = £71,520.17   (L + M)

(O) Department Profit = £39,477.79   (J - N)
(P) Department Profit % = 29.20%   (O ÷ H x 100)

(Q) Utilisation = 85.00%   (C ÷ B x 100)
(R) Productivity = 112.00%   (A ÷ C x 100)
(S) Overall Efficiency = 95.20%   (A ÷ B x 100)

Calculating The Gain In Your Utilisation

The Effects of a 6% Increase in Utilisation

(A)	Hours Sold	=	2,242.24	(C x R)
(B)	Hours Attended	=	2,200.00	
(C)	Hours Worked	=	2,002.00	(B x Q)
(D)	Hours Idle Time	=	198.00	(B - C)
(E)	Recovery Rate	=	£64.56	
(F)	N° of Technicians	=	10	
(G)	Average Labour Cost	=	£12.95	
(H)	Labour Sales	=	£144,759.01	(A x E)
(I)	Labour Cost of Sales	=	£25,925.90	(C x G)
(J)	Labour Gross Profit	=	£118,833.11	(H - I)
(K)	Gross Profit %	=	82.09%	(J ÷ H x 100)
(L)	Cost of Idle Time	=	£2,564.10	(D x G)
(M)	All Other Expenses	=	£67,246.67	
(N)	Department Expenses	=	£69,810.77	(L + M)
(O)	Department Profit	=	£49,022.34	(J - N)
(P)	Department Profit %	=	33.86%	(O ÷ H x 100)
(Q)	Utilisation	=	91.00%	(C ÷ B x 100)
(R)	Productivity	=	112.00%	(A ÷ C x 100)
(S)	Overall Efficiency	=	101.92%	(A ÷ B x 100)
(T)	Monthly Profit Gain	=	£9,544.55	
(U)	**Annual Profit Gain**	=	**£114,534.60**	(T x 12)

Now try this with your own department to see how much more profit you can realise by increasing your Utilisation.

KEEP IT ON TRACK

Now that you know how to calculate Utilisation and how to forecast the profit gains, you will obviously want to track your results by measuring the trends on an ongoing basis. Keep in mind that it is the *trend* of your performance that is far more meaningful than a one-off snap shot.

It is important to understand that Utilisation does not affect your Labour Gross Profit %. It is your Recovery Rate and your Productivity that makes a difference to that Key Performance Area. Utilisation is not measuring how long it takes to complete a job; it is measuring how much of the available time is being used. It is the relationship between Hours Attended and the Hours Worked. In other words, how much of your Technicians *available* time is being utilised.

If your Accountant does not correctly identify the differences between Hours Worked and Idle Time, and calculates your Labour Cost of Sales as your Technicians salary, then your Labour Gross Profit will be adversely affected, which will give you an incorrect Labour Gross Profit figure This is a very dangerous scenario because your Labour Gross Profit would be reporting much lower than it otherwise would be and Utilisation would be reported at 100%.

The real danger here is that you are blind to any adverse trends in your Utilisation and Labour Gross Profit % and you may make wrong decisions based on that information. These statistics are only brought into view when they are calculated correctly.

After reading this chapter you might come to the conclusion that a few changes are necessary within your accounting methods and making changes are sometimes painful and may take more effort than you are willing to employ. But if you want to make the right decisions within your business, you have to have the right information because you cannot make a good decision with bad information.

Your management accounts are like a special kind of map in that they tell you where you are now. When you read them, you make up your mind whether you want to stay there or go somewhere else. In most cases you will want to improve your results, which means that you want to go elsewhere, but if your starting point is incorrect what chance do you have of getting to where you really want to be?

* * * * *

To conclude this chapter, I'll leave you with this one final thought. Understand the words of Michelangelo in the opening quotation and make use of this 7-step process to realise the gains that you can make in your Service Department. The constant vision of the additional profit you can make will keep you motivated to achieve greater things providing that you plan your route *before* you embark upon your journey because you need to ensure that the end justifies the means.

> *"It is not the going out of the port*
> *but the coming in with the prize,*
> *that determines the success of your voyage."*

Chapter VIII

Calculating The Gain
In Your Productivity

*"Start by doing what is necessary;
then do what is possible;
and suddenly you are doing the impossible"*

- St. Francis of Assisi

Chapter VIII

Calculating The Gain In Your Productivity

Productivity is the relationship between Hours Sold and Hours Worked. The Hours Sold are influenced by customer-facing staff and the Hours Worked are influenced by your Technicians abilities to beat the allocated job times. Therefore when you plan to improve your Productivity you need to understand by what method you are going to achieve the increase because the effects upon your profitability are very different. This chapter will show how to calculate improvement in both areas and the effects that each change will have upon your financial reports.

Increasing your Productivity by increasing the Hours Sold will improve your profitability, but improving your Productivity by reducing the Hours Worked will not improve your profitability. If you are unsure of why this is so, you can get the full information from Chapter III. When you feel comfortable that you fully understand this concept you are ready to proceed with this chapter.

Where Are You Now?
Calculating Productivity from your results is very easy and if you are fortunate, your management accounts may already have this key performance indicator present. However, if you need to calculate your result manually here's a quick reminder:

(A) Hours Sold   = 1,146.2
(B) Hours Worked = 1,042
(C) **Productivity** = **110%**   (A ÷ B x 100)

In this example you can see that the front counter staff have sold 1,146.2 hours and the Technicians have completed those jobs in 1,042 hours, which means that the Productivity is 110%.

WHERE DO YOU WANT TO BE?

Firstly, you need to decide upon the level of increase you think that you can realistically achieve with your Productivity. You can forecast how many more hours you need to sell to reach your target and then you can calculate how much more profit you can make from the actions you are considering. There is no point implementing actions if they are not going to deliver enough profit so it is best to calculate the amount of profit you will make *before* you implement your actions.

When you improve your Productivity by increasing the Hours Sold a number of things will change such as Labour Sales, and let's not forget about the increases in your profit. The question is how do you calculate these changes so that you know what is going to happen well in advance?

When you look at a whole page of figures they can be daunting, so to help you, here is the simple 7-step system that makes the whole planning process easy to understand. Firstly, let's begin by understanding what happens when your customer-facing staff improve your Productivity by increasing the number of Hours Sold.

CALCULATING IMPROVEMENT: OPTION 1

To get started let's create a small business called Insight Motors and use their statistics as a working example. When you understand the process for yourself you can replace the figures with your own. Here are the figures for Insight Motors:

(A) Hours Sold   = 2,094.40
(B) Hours Worked = 1,870
(C) Hours Attended = 2,200
(D) Idle Time   = 330   (C - B)
(E) **Productivity** = **112%**   (A ÷ B x 100)

The benchmark for Productivity is 110% to 125%, which means that Insight Motors certainly have plenty of room for improvement. Now let's see what happens when you improve your Productivity by increasing the Hours Sold.

STEP 1: INCREASE THE HOURS SOLD

Productivity at 112% is at the low end of the benchmark so for the purpose of this exercise, let's make a decision to set a target of 118%, which is an increase in Productivity of 6%. In this exercise, the increase in Productivity will be achieved by increasing the Hours Sold as opposed to beating the allocated job times.

Now that you know what you want to achieve, you can begin with your process of improvement. As you will see, it's not simply a matter of increasing your profit by 6% because other things change too such as Labour Sales and Overall Efficiency. To get started with the process you first obtain the revised number of Hours Sold by multiplying the number of Hours

Calculating The Gain In Your Productivity

Worked by your revised Productivity target figure. For example, the number of Hours Worked is currently being reported at 1,870 and to establish the revised number of Hours Sold you simply multiply this figure by your Productivity target figure.

Hours Worked x Productivity ÷ 100 = Hours Sold

1,870 x 118 ÷ 100 = 2,206.6

	Current	Improved
Hours Attended	2,200	2,200
Hours Worked	1,870	1,870
Idle Time	330	330
Productivity	112%	118%
Hours Sold	**2,094.40** ⇨	**2,206.60**

You can see from this example that the Hours Attended have remained constant because they do not affect your Productivity. You can also see that the Hours Worked have remained constant because the Technicians have spent the same amount of time clocked onto the jobs and therefore the amount of Idle Time also remains constant; those areas are affected by your Utilisation. The increase in Productivity has come from the customer-facing people who have increased the number of Hours Sold.

STEP 2: INCREASE LABOUR SALES

Now that you have increased the Hours Sold, how much revenue are they worth to you? To answer this question, you need to establish the value of Labour Sales which is calculated by taking the number of Hours Sold and multiplying this figure by your Labour Recovery Rate. Take care here; the increase is not to be calculated by using your Charge Out rate because discounts are often given and this would give you an overstated figure. Your Recovery Rate is the figure to use here because this is the figure after discounts have been given.

Ideally, you would use the Hours Sold and the Recovery Rate for each income sector such as retail, warranty and internal to give you a more accurate and meaningful figure as in the example below.

	Hrs. Sold	Recovery Rate
Retail	1050	£69.20
Warranty	160	£57.48
Internal	290	£67.50

For the sake of simplicity, the following model uses the Total Hours Sold and the average Recovery Rate; only you can decide which is right for your purposes.

In the example below, Insight Motors are reporting their average Labour Recovery Rate at £64.56 so the increase in Labour Sales can now be calculated as follows:

Hours Sold x Recovery Rate = Labour Sales

2,206.6 x 64.56 = 142,458.10

	Current	Improved
Hours Sold	2,094.40	2,206.6
Recovery Rate	£64.56	£64.56
Labour Sales	**£135,214.46**	⇨ **£142,458.10**

Here you can see the additional revenue that has been generated from the increased number of Hours Sold. Naturally, you will also make more profit from Oil Sales, Sub Let and any other services that you offer, but again for the sake of simplicity, these items have been omitted so that you can see the effects of Productivity in isolation. However, now that you have increased the Hours Sold and Labour Sales, how much money has it cost you to complete this task? In other words, does the end justify the means?

STEP 3: LABOUR COST OF SALES

To calculate how much the increases in performance have cost you, you need to calculate your Labour Cost of Sales. This is the part of the Service Department that causes the most confusion. The Labour Cost of Sales refers only to the Hours Worked and not the Hours Attended. The cost of any attended time that has not been worked is classified as Idle Time and is shown within your expenses.

The Labour Cost of Sales is calculated by taking the number of Hours Worked and multiplying this figure by the average amount of money that you pay to your Technicians per hour attended. The money paid to your Technicians is called the Average Labour Cost.

Insight Motors are reporting their Average Labour Cost at £12.95 per hour. This is the average amount of money paid to each Technician per hour. If you have any incentive or bonus schemes in place you will need to include these payments within your Average Labour Cost.

Now that you have this figure, you can re-calculate the Labour Cost of Sales as follows:

Hrs Wkd x Av. Lab. Cost = Lab. Cost of Sales

1,870 x 12.95 = 24,216.50

	Current		Improved
Hours Worked	1,870		1,870
Av. Labour Cost	£12.95		£12.95
Cost of Sales	**£24,216.50**	⇨	**£24,216.50**

Here you can see that the Labour Cost of Sales has remained constant because the number of Hours Worked has remained constant. Although there is no change here it is an important point to keep in mind because you need to understand how this affects your operational performance.

Carefully review the figures below and ensure that you fully understand the logic within each step before you continue reading.

	Current		Improved
Productivity	112%	⇨	118%
Hours Sold	2,094.40	⇨	2,206.6
Hours Attended	2,200		2,200
Hours Worked	1,870	⇨	1,870
Hours Idle Time	330		330
Recovery Rate	£64.56		£64.56
Av. Labour Cost	£12.95		£12.95
Labour Sales	£135,214.46	⇨	£142,458.10
Cost of Sales	£24,216.50	⇨	£24,216.50

STEP 4: CALCULATE LABOUR GROSS PROFIT
Profit is measured at two different points within all businesses and the first profit measurement is called Gross Profit.

The term "Gross" literally means "without deduction" therefore calculating the Gross Profit of any product is simply Sales minus Cost of Sales *before* any expenses are taken into account. Because Idle Time is an expense, you can now see why it is so important to exclude it from the Labour Cost of Sales. In this example, you are only measuring the effects upon Labour Gross Profit and so the formula is simply:

Lab. Sales − Lab. Cost of Sales = Labour GP

	Current	Improved
Labour Sales	£135,214.46	£142,458.10
Cost of Sales	£24,216.50	£24,216.50
Labour G.P.	**£110,997.96** ⇨	**£118,241.60**

Now you can see that the Labour Gross Profit has increased by £7,243.64. However, to understand what has happened in real terms you need to calculate the Labour Gross Profit % which is calculated as follows:

Labour GP ÷ Labour Sales x 100 = Labour GP%

	Current	Improved
Labour Sales	£135,214.46	£142,458.10
Cost of Sales	£24,216.50	£24,216.50
Labour G.P.	£110,997.96	£118,241.60
Labour GP%	**82.09%** ⇨	**83.00%**

Here you can see that the Labour Gross Profit% has increased by almost 1% which confirms that when you improve your Productivity by increasing the Hours Sold you will see an increase in your Labour Gross Profit. This is an important factor to remember because you may recall from the previous chapter that when you increase your Utilisation there is no change in your Labour Gross Profit%.

Once again, now you can see the importance of calculating your Labour Cost of Sales correctly because Utilisation does *not* affect your Labour Gross Profit % but Productivity does.

The baseline for Labour Gross Profit is to be greater than 75%, but before you make any judgements on this figure, first make sure that your Accountant is putting your figures in the right places on your management accounts or you could be drawn into making wrong decisions about your profitability. More information on this subject is contained within the previous chapter.

At this stage of the process you have calculated everything up to the point of Labour Gross Profit, but have you incurred any expenses along the way?

Within a department there are two types of expenses; those triggered by sales volume and those that are not triggered by sales volume. Direct Expenses are only accumulated when you sell something and In-Direct Expenses are evident whether you sell anything or not. In this exercise the Hours Sold have changed but the Hours Worked have not changed therefore Idle Time will not have changed. The only increases that you will see in your expenses are the small amounts that you pay for consumables. There will be no increases in salaries and wages and no increases in Idle Time because the Hours Worked have remained constant and so in this scenario the departmental expenses need no further recalculation.

STEP 5: CALCULATE DEPARTMENTAL PROFIT
Departmental Profit is the final calculation in the accounting process for the Service Department and it is also known as the bottom line, Operating Profit or Direct Profit.

If Gross Profit is the calculation *before* Expenses have been taken into account, then Departmental Profit is the calculation *after* Expenses have been taken into account. The formula for Departmental Profit is simply:

Gross Profit minus all Departmental Expenses

	Current	Improved
Labour Sales	£135,214.46	£142,458.10
Cost of Sales	£24,216.50	£24,216.50
Labour G.P.	£110,997.96	£118,241.60
Labour GP%	82.09%	83.00%
Expenses	£71,520.17	£71,520.17
Dept. Profit	**£39,477.79** ⇨	**£46,721.43**

Here you can see that the Departmental Profit has increased by £7,243.64 but you need to know if it has been increased in real terms, or in other words, has the Departmental Profit increased as a percentage, or have we been busy fools?

Departmental Profit ÷ Labour Sales Value x 100

	Current	Improved
Labour Sales	£135,214.46	£142,458.10
Cost of Sales	£24,216.50	£24,216.50
Labour G.P.	£110,997.96	£118,241.60
Labour GP%	82.09%	83.00%
Expenses	£71,520.17	£71,520.17
Dept. Profit	£39,477.79	£46,721.43
Dept. Profit %	**29.20%** ⇨	**32.80%**

Now you can see that the Departmental Profit % has increased to 32.80% which shows a real profit growth of 3.60% so the end result certainly does justify putting more effort into this area of your operational performance. In conclusion, when you improve your Productivity by increasing the number of Hours Sold you will see the effects of your work in the following areas on your management accounts:

Summary of Effects

Hours Attended	⇨	**No Change**
Hours Sold	⇨	**Increase**
Hours Worked	⇨	**No Change**
Productivity	⇨	**Increase**
Utilisation	⇨	**No Change**
Overall Efficiency	⇨	**Increase**
Labour Sales	⇨	**Increase**
Cost of Sales	⇨	**No Change**
Labour G.P.	⇨	**Increase**
Labour GP%	⇨	**Increase**
Expenses	⇨	**No Change**
Dept. Profit	⇨	**Increase**
Dept. Profit %	⇨	**Increase**

Calculating The Gain In Your Productivity

Before the change in operational performance

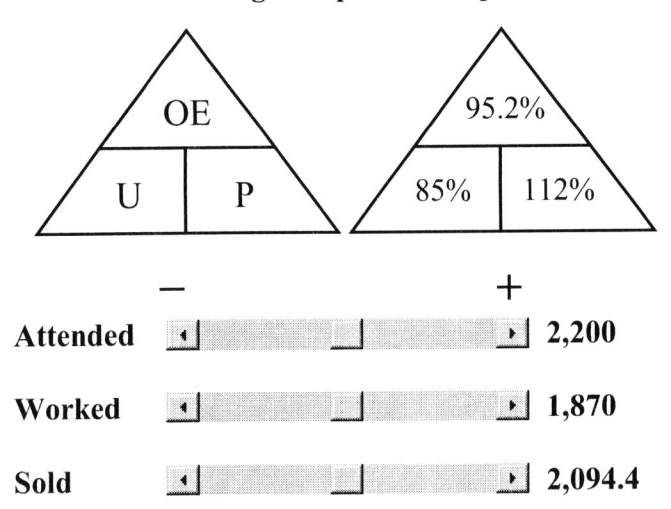

```
      OE                      95.2%
   U     P               85%      112%
```

                −   +

Attended ◁ ▭ ▷ **2,200**

Worked ◁ ▭ ▷ **1,870**

Sold ◁ ▭ ▷ **2,094.4**

After the change in operational performance

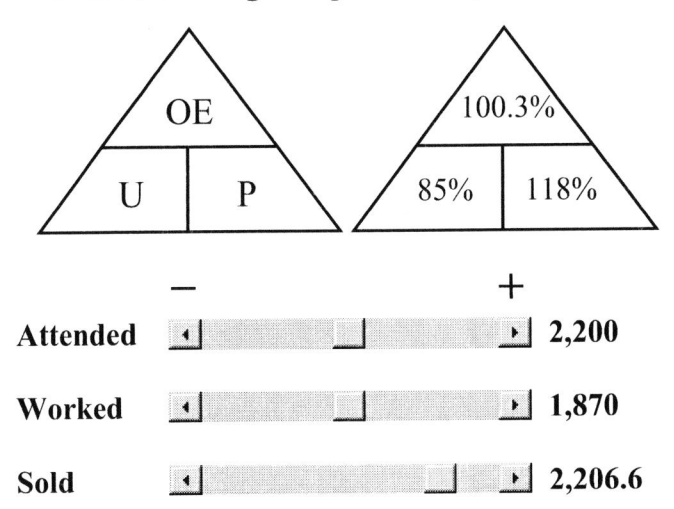

```
      OE                     100.3%
   U     P               85%      118%
```

                  −   +

Attended ◁ ▭ ▷ **2,200**

Worked ◁ ▭ ▷ **1,870**

Sold ◁ ▭ ▷ **2,206.6**

Remember that these gains are produced by your customer-facing staff selling more hours and not by the Technicians beating the allocated job times.

CALCULATING IMPROVEMENT: OPTION 2

Now let's understand what happens when you improve your Productivity by your Technicians beating the allocated job times.

To maintain simplicity we'll use the same business model as in the previous section as a working example. Once again, when you understand the process for yourself you can replace the figures with your own. Here are the figures for Insight Motors:

(A) Hours Sold   = 2,094.40
(B) Hours Worked = 1,870
(C) Hours Attended = 2,200
(D) Idle Time   = 330   (C - B)
(E) **Productivity** = **112%**   (A ÷ B x 100)

The benchmark for Productivity is 110% to 125%, which means that Insight Motors certainly have plenty of room for improvement. Now let's see what happens to these statistics and your management accounts when you improve your Productivity to 118% by beating the allocated job times.

STEP 1: REDUCE THE HOURS WORKED

Productivity at 112% is at the low end of the benchmark so for the purpose of this exercise, let's make a decision to set a target of 118% just as in the previous section, which is an increase in Productivity of 6%.

The effects in your operational performance in this exercise will be different to the previous section because the increase in Productivity will be achieved by your Technicians beating the allocated job times as opposed to your customer-facing staff increasing the Hours Sold. Because the Hours Sold remain the same, the Labour Sales will remain the same at £135,214.46

In this exercise, your Technicians will be completing the jobs quicker and therefore you will be reducing the Hours Worked. You calculate this as follows:

Hours Sold ÷ Productivity x 100 = Hours Worked

	Current		Improved
Hours Sold	2,094.40		2,094.40
Productivity	**112%**	⇨	**118%**
Hours Worked	**1,870**	⇨	**1,774.91**

Here you can see that the Technicians have been completing the jobs in a quicker time and therefore the Hours Worked have reduced to 1,774.91 which is an improvement of 95.09 hours. However, what you have to consider in this instance is that no more work has been put into the time that has been saved and the workshop begins to run out of work before the end of the working day so now you have to think about the consequences of this action.

Firstly, because Hours Sold have not increased there is no additional income therefore there will be no change in the Labour Sales at £135,214.46, but what will happen to the Labour Cost of Sales.

STEP 2: LABOUR COST OF SALES

Labour Cost of Sales refers to the amount of money that you pay to your Technicians for the amount of time that they have been clocked onto jobs to produce the Hours Sold. In this instance, the Technicians have spent less time clocked onto jobs because they are beating the allocated job times and so the Labour Cost of Sales will therefore reduce because the Hours Worked have reduced. Yes, you still have to pay your Technicians their full salary but the difference between what you pay for the Hours Worked and the Hours Attended is shown in your Idle Time.

The Labour Cost of Sales is calculated by taking the number of Hours Worked and multiplying this figure by the average amount of money that you pay your Technicians per hour attended. The money paid to your Technicians is called the Average Labour Cost.

Insight Motors are reporting their Average Labour Cost at £12.95 per hour. This is the average amount of money paid to each Technician per hour. Now that you have this figure, you can re-calculate the Labour Cost of Sales as follows:

Hrs Wkd x Av. Lab. Cost = Labour Cost of Sales

	Current	Improved
Hours Worked	1,870	1,774.91
Av. Labour Cost	£12.95	£12.95
Lab. Cost of Sales	**£24,216.50** ⇨	**£22,985.08**

You can see from this illustration that the Labour Cost of Sales has reduced because the Hours Worked have reduced which represents a reduction in the Labour Cost of Sales to the value of £1,231.42.

So far this is excellent news because you are continuing to sell the same number of hours for the same value but now the cost of those hours has been reduced therefore you must have a higher Gross Profit on those hours that have been sold.

STEP 3: LABOUR GROSS PROFIT

The term "Gross" literally means "without deduction" therefore calculating the Gross Profit of any product is simply Sales minus Cost of Sales *before* any expenses are taken into account. Because Idle Time is an expense, now you can see why it is so important to exclude it from the Labour Cost of Sales.

In this example, you are measuring the effects upon Labour Gross Profit and so the formula is simply:

Labour Sales - Labour Cost of Sales = Labour GP.

	Current	Improved
Labour Sales	£135,214.46	£135,214.46
Cost of Sales	£24,216.50	£22,985.08
Labour G.P.	**£110,997.96** ⇨	**£112,229.38**

Now you can see that the Labour Gross Profit has improved by £1,231.42, which is the result of the gain in the Labour Cost of Sales. However, to understand what has happened in real terms you need to calculate the Labour Gross Profit %, which is calculated as follows:

Labour GP ÷ Labour Sales x 100 = Labour GP%

	Current	Improved
Labour Sales	£135,214.46	£135,214.46
Cost of Sales	£24,216.50	£22,985.08
Labour G.P.	£110,997.96	£112,229.38
Labour GP%	**82.09%** ⇨	**83.00%**

Here you can see that the Labour Gross Profit % has increased by almost 1% which confirms that when you improve your Productivity by beating the allocated job times you will see an increase in both your Labour Gross Profit and your Labour Gross Profit %. This is an important factor to remember because you may recall from the previous chapter that when you increase your Utilisation there is no change in your Labour Gross Profit %.

Now you know that if you want to influence your Labour Gross Profit %, beating the allocated job times will provide the results that you require. However, you may have noticed that you obtain a much bigger gain in Labour Gross Profit when you improve your Productivity by increasing the Hours Sold as opposed to beating the job times.

The baseline for Labour Gross Profit is to be greater than 75%, but before you make any judgements on this figure, first make sure that your Accountant is putting your figures in the right places on your management accounts or you could be drawn into making wrong decisions about your profitability. The allocation of Idle Time is of course a significant factor in these calculations and in your interpretation of these key performance indicators.

STEP 4: EXPENSES AND IDLE TIME

Within a department there are two types of expenses; those triggered by sales volume and those that are not triggered by sales volume. Direct Expenses are only accumulated when you sell something and In-Direct Expenses are evident whether you sell anything or not. Idle Time is a Direct Expense.

Calculating The Gain In Your Productivity

For the purposes of this illustration only Idle Time is separated from all other expenses so that you can clearly see the effects of the change in your Productivity because most other expenses (apart from Consumables) will remain constant. Firstly, you need to assess what has happened to the amount of Idle Time and the calculation is as follows:

Hours Attended – Hours Worked = Hours Idle

	Current	Improved
Hours Attended	2,200	2,200
Hours Worked	1,870	1,774.91
Hours Idle Time	**330** ⇨	**425.09**

Here you can see that the amount of Idle Time has increased by 95.09 hours because the Technicians have spent 95.09 fewer hours clocked on to the jobs. In other words, this is how much quicker they have completed the jobs.

Remember that the Hours Worked affects your Productivity and also your Idle Time. In this instance, no further jobs have been booked into the workshop to capitalise on the saved time and so Idle Time increases. The balancing effect between Hours Worked and Idle Time can be seen more clearly in the illustrations on the following page.

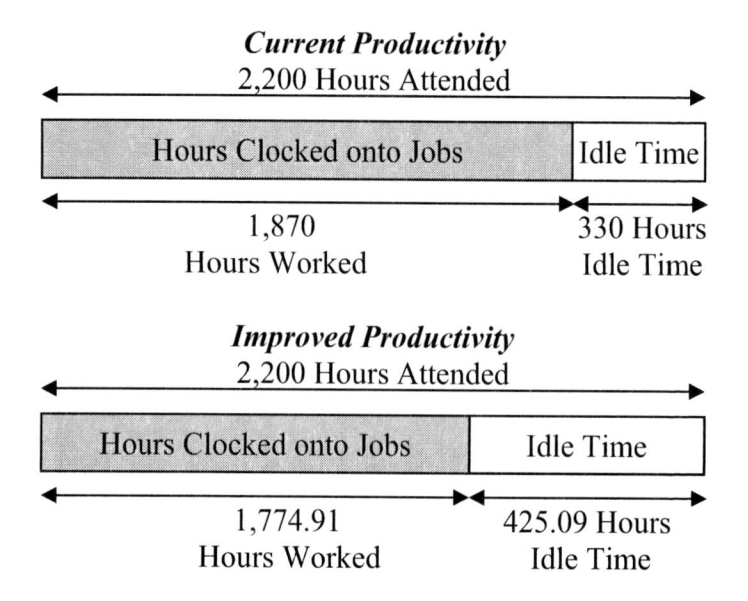

Current Productivity
2,200 Hours Attended

Hours Clocked onto Jobs	Idle Time
1,870 Hours Worked	330 Hours Idle Time

Improved Productivity
2,200 Hours Attended

Hours Clocked onto Jobs	Idle Time
1,774.91 Hours Worked	425.09 Hours Idle Time

Now you know that Idle Time has increased, it's time to discover how much money it has cost you. The calculation for the cost of Idle Time is as follows:

Hours Idle x Av. Labour Cost = Idle Time

	Current	Improved
Hours Idle Time	330	425.09
Av. Labour Cost	£12.95	£12.95
Cost of Idle Time	**£4,273.50** ⇨	**£5,504.92**

Here you can see that the cost of Idle Time has increased by £1,231.42 If this figure looks a little familiar to you it's because you have seen it before. This figure in Idle Time equates exactly to the figure that was calculated for the increase in Labour Gross Profit in Step 3. Departmental Expenses have now increased from £71,520.17 to £72,751.59. This is a significant point to understand!

When you improve your Productivity by beating the allocated job times all that you do is shift the balance between Hours Worked and Idle Time so there is no real gain. Yes, you increase the Gross Profit on those *particular* jobs, but not on the department as a whole.

Unless you fill the time you have saved with another job, which means increasing your Utilisation, the time you have saved falls into Idle Time and the cost of that is identical to the increase in the Gross Profit.

However, just a thought, you could be even worse off if you are paying a time-saved Productivity bonus to your Technicians because your Labour Cost of Sales would increase by the value of your bonus payment.

STEP 5: CALCULATE DEPARTMENTAL PROFIT

Departmental Profit is the final calculation in the accounting process for the Service Department and it is also known as the bottom line, Operating Profit or Direct Profit. This is the point at which you discover whether your efforts have been worthwhile.

If Gross Profit is the calculation *before* Expenses have been taken into account, then Departmental Profit is the calculation *after* Expenses have been taken into account.

In this example other sales such as oil, lubricants and consumables have been omitted so that you can see the effects of your Productivity in isolation. The formula for Departmental Profit is simply:

Gross Profit minus all Departmental Expenses

	Current	Improved
Gross Profit	£110,997.96	£112,229.38
Dept. Expenses	£71,520.17	£72,751.59
Dept. Profit	**£39,477.79** ⇨	**£39,477.79**

Here you can see the evidence that the Departmental Profit has not changed. In conclusion then, you have to admit that simply beating the allocated job times is not all it's cracked up to be. Yes, it is worth doing, but not by itself; you must capitalise on the extra time that you save by increasing your Utilisation *at the same time* otherwise all of your gain gets eaten up in your expenses as Idle Time.

When you improve your Productivity by beating the allocated job times, the Gross Profit on *those particular jobs* increase, but the gain gets eroded away by expenses.

On the following page you can see an illustration of the Law of The Service Department so that you can see how improving your Productivity in this way affects your operational performance.

Calculating The Gain In Your Productivity

Before the change in operational performance

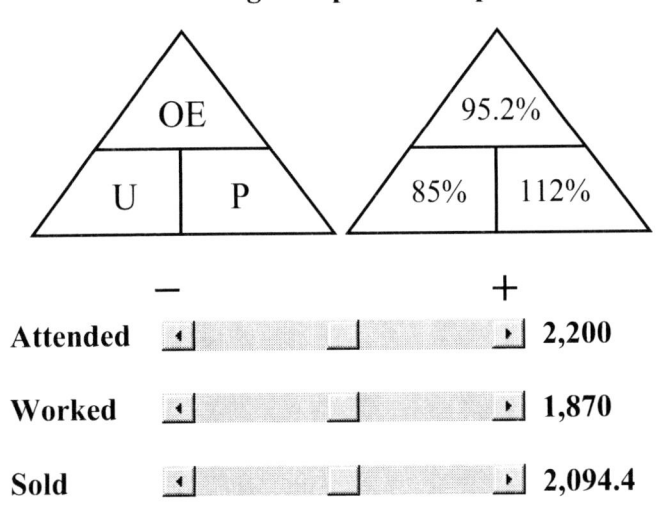

```
      /\                    /\
     /OE\                  /95.2%\
    /----\                /--------\
   /U  | P\              /85% | 112%\
  /____|___\            /_____|_____\
```

              −   +

Attended ◄ ▬▬▬▬▬▬▬▬▬ ► 2,200

Worked ◄ ▬▬▬▬▬▬▬▬▬ ► 1,870

Sold ◄ ▬▬▬▬▬▬▬▬▬ ► 2,094.4

After the change in operational performance

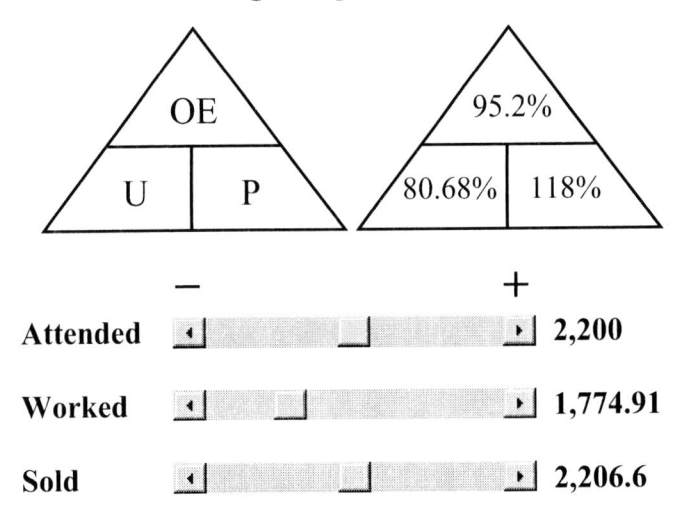

```
      /\                    /\
     /OE\                  /95.2%\
    /----\                /--------\
   /U  | P\              /80.68%|118%\
  /____|___\            /_____|_____\
```

              −   +

Attended ◄ ▬▬▬▬▬▬▬▬▬ ► 2,200

Worked ◄ ▬▬▬▬▬▬▬▬▬ ► 1,774.91

Sold ◄ ▬▬▬▬▬▬▬▬▬ ► 2,206.6

Remember that the Hours Worked are common to both Productivity and Utilisation therefore as you change one you automatically change the other.

Productivity is a great profit builder, but only if you understand the full effects of its behaviour upon your operational performance.

You have seen in this chapter that the real profit gains come from your customer-facing staff having the ability to maintain or increase the number of Hours Sold. However, if you were to ask your team to write down their job descriptions, how many of them would write "to sell hours"? In many cases most of the efforts are placed upon the Technicians beating the job times and the workshop runs out of work before the end of the day because the time that has been saved has not been utilised effectively.

* * * * *

To conclude this chapter, I'll leave you with this one final thought. In the real world, improving your Productivity is a combination of the efforts of your customer-facing staff selling hours and your Technicians beating the job times, and again in the real world it is up to you to control and understand the effects of each of these actions upon your operational performance. If you're running in the wrong direction, more speed won't help.

"When you control the ball, you control the score."

- Pele

Where To Now?

*"Success is a journey
not a destination."*

WHERE TO NOW?

One of the most recognised and respected awards in the martial art of Karate is of course the Black Belt. It is seen by many as the ultimate prize in its field, but for the holder of this accolade the journey does not end here. The techniques they have mastered must be practised until they become second-nature and their actions become smooth, effortless and instinctive. Once perfected, the task of the master is to pass on their skills so that others may benefit.

It takes years of practise, dedication and training to attain the coveted Black Belt, but there are a number of other belts to be won along the journey that provide the necessary recognition and motivation to continue. And so it is the same with your Service Department.

The art of achieving mastery with these three key performance indictors is to set yourself a long-term goal, a Black Belt if you will, and then to set sub goals along the way which recognise that you are moving your career in the right direction and providing you with the necessary motivation to continue.

One of the key factors in the journey ahead of you is to ensure that you have the right information from your Accountant so that you can accurately monitor the actions that you are implementing into your business. You cannot make the right decisions with the wrong information. Management accounts are for the benefit of your Service Department, not for the benefit of the Accounts Department. Your accounts must be tailored to reflect what is happening within your Department otherwise they are worthless.

There are around two hundred key performance indicators in the Motor Industry and this book covers just three of them, but it is these three powerful key performance indicators that ultimately control the direction and the profitability of your workshop. Although they make take you only a few minutes to learn, they take a lifetime to master.

To reach the top of your profession you will need plenty of practise, dedication and training to help you on your way and then you will need to continue with daily monitoring if you are to *stay* at the top of your profession. As the opening quotation states, *success is a journey, not a destination.*

Perhaps the most important discipline of all in your recipe for success is practise. You will need to learn these three key performance indicators until they become second-nature and your thoughts and actions upon them are smooth, effortless and instinctive.

When you see more than three days lead time, what you actually see is an opportunity to increase your Utilisation. When you see your work-in-progress increasing, what you actually see in an opportunity to increase your Productivity. Before you implement actions into your business you need to be able to visualise the effects that these actions will have upon your operational performance and how they relate to The Law of The Service Department. When you are able see opportunities and translate your thoughts instinctively in these terms you will know that you are heading in the direction of making a more profitable business. It's just a matter of practise.

Practise is just another way of saying that you should not expect to get everything right first time. You need to be bold and try something new once in a while and you should not be afraid of making a few mistakes; that's how real life works. It could be said that if you do not make any mistakes in your career you are not trying hard enough.

Amateurs practise until they get it right;
Professionals practise until they can't get it wrong.

Practise means taking action and it is the act of doing something that generates more profit for you and creates change in your business. Few people like the process of change, but it is the only thing that brings progress. When it comes to embracing the challenge of change there are just three types of people:

1. Those that make change happen
2. Those that let change happen
3. Those that say "What happened?"

Taking action is the one thing that separates a good businessman from a great businessman. Many people see opportunities in their life, but only a few people do something about it.

The things that come to those who wait
are what's left behind by those who got there first.

Where To Now?

To conclude this chapter I'll leave you with a few final thoughts. If you truly want to make a difference to the profitability of your business *and* the quality of your life you must take action now. Knowing what to do is not enough, you must *do* what you know.

Use the spaces provided in this book to keep a record of your *actions*, not your thoughts, hopes and wishes because it is what you *do* that counts, and believe me, everything counts.

Be inspired and take action everyday, even if it is only a small action. Developing the habit of doing something everyday extends your abilities and stretches your awareness. Remember that the longest journey begins with a single step. The act of getting started is one of the most important acts of all.

I wish you every success for the future and if I can help you in anyway please contact me by email, but now that you have all of this information perhaps the most important message that I can leave with you is this:

> *"Knowing and not doing*
> *is worse than not knowing at all."*

- Jeff Smith

You have now reached the end of "How To Make More Profit With Your Service Department", or is this just the beginning?

What happens if we buy Jeff Smith's books for all of our managers and then they leave us?
What happens if we don't... and they stay?
PROFIT

*"It's not companies who are successful…
It's the people working within them."*

The one problem with this book is that if you lend it out to a friend, you will never get it back! Naturally, you will want to keep your copy to yourself for safe keeping so that you know where to find it at that critical time when you need it most and to keep track of your own personal development.

You can obtain further copies for other people in your organisation by contacting one of the following:

To order by telephone in the UK:
01384 371432

To order by telephone outside of the UK:
0044 1384 371432

Email:
KPI@AskInsight.com

Visit our web site
www.AskInsight.com

Insight

Insight Training & Development Ltd
Publications Department (SB)
P. O. Box 1234
Stourbridge
England
DY8 2GE

Books by Jeff Smith

There are around two hundred KPIs currently in use within the Motor industry and to operate you business effectively you are expected to know them all.

This book has been written because everyone working with Key Performance Indicators needs a central point of reference; something that gives you the information you want in less than two minutes.

"This book is quality. I believe it is absolutely essential to everyone in the Motor Industry."

Professor Garel Rhys OBE
Director of the Centre of Automotive Industry Research
Cardiff University Business School.

The K.P.I Book
The ultimate guide to understanding the
Key Performance Indicators of your business

Produced in hardback and published in 2001
Reprinted in 2001, 2002, 2003, 2004, 2005, 2006

ISBN 0-9540259-0-3

To order by telephone in the UK:
01384 371432

To order by telephone outside of the UK:
0044 1384 371432

Email:
KPI@AskInsight.com

Visit our web site for a FREE sample
www.AskInsight.com

To order by mail:

Insight

Insight Training & Development Ltd
Publications Department (SB)
P. O. Box 1234
Stourbridge
England
DY8 2GE

Books by Jeff Smith

For further information on books written by
Jeff Smith please visit our website at
www.AskInsight.com